AuthorHouse™
1663 Liberty Drive
Bloomington, IN 47403
www.authorhouse.com
Phone: 1-800-839-8640

First published by AuthorHouse 08/19/2009

ISBN: 978-1-4490-2030-9

Library Congress Number: 2009908616

Printed in the United States of America
Bloomington, Indiana

This book is printed on acid-free paper.

authorHOUSE®

Living Well at One Hundred

Darlene McCord, Ph.D., FAPWCA

ACKNOWLEDGEMENTS

Over the years, special people have entered my life, just as they were needed, to help bring me to where I am today. I will call attention to some of them here in my Acknowledgements. However, the true blessings in my life come from tens-of-thousands of patients who have used my products to treat their skin diseases and wounds. Hundreds of these patients have personally let me know how much my products have helped. My work and the rewards associated with knowing that each day I am helping improve the quality of life for patients is fundamental to who I am today. This book is my way of reaching out to more people and trying to bring them knowledge that may improve or save their lives. I hope you are one of them.

My work requires long hours and dedication to a vision that drives me. This time and energy would not be available if it were not for my husband, Dr. James B. McCord. He has allowed me to dream big and reach for the stars. He has been not only a guiding light through the good times; he has lit my path when no one else was around. To you, dear husband, I say thanks.

Writing a book requires a team of people, especially a first book. I thank my editors, Sharon Yamato and Kelli Andresen. Their attention to detail and structure ensured that the book had clarity of message, and to Nicole Nisly, MD, who supported their work. She spent hours on the first drafts of the book checking for small details that contributed to an improved presentation of the facts and details. Finally, I want to thank the design team that created the book. Thomas Sulentic and Serina Brekke made the book come alive with the selection of photos, exciting page layouts, and easy to follow charts. To one and all, thanks.

To you, the reader, I want to say thanks for taking the time to follow along with me on this journey. The journey to good health is a meaningful voyage and every choice matters.

Table of Contents

I choose to risk my significance so that which came to me as seed goes to the next as blossom, and that which came to me as blossom, goes on as fruit.

—Dawna Markova

INTRODUCTION

This book was borne out of the same fundamental necessity that has fueled many other books and endless Internet sites. Whether you have been diagnosed with a disease such as cancer, atherosclerosis, or diabetes, or you are simply undergoing the process of aging, the answers to medical questions are very individual. The sad fact is that most of us can no longer turn to our physicians exclusively to get complete advice.

I have read countless books and spent hundreds of hours perusing the Internet, and one thing I have learned is that millions of people are looking for answers to their medical questions—and many of these answers can be found outside of their physicians' offices. Perhaps the main reason for this quest over the past few years is that many of us now realize that we only visit our physician when something is wrong with us—most of us do not go to a doctor's office to get started on a healthy lifestyle track. Currently most physicians are not trained in nutrition, and many do not even support the use of supplements, regardless of the overwhelming scientific evidence about the benefits of supplement use. The good news is that a new breed of physician is emerging. Integrative and functional medical doctors are focused on healthy lifestyle medicine.

This book offers a simple, straightforward approach to living well at one hundred°. While this concept has many meanings, we choose to look at it as a "way" of not only living disease-free, but as a "way" of living as naturally and vitally as possible. The book's focus is on achieving wellness and avoiding illness.

Over the past century, the average life expectancy has more than doubled. The extension of human longevity is one of our greatest human achievements. While the understanding of and implementation of good hygiene practices has played a major role in reducing deaths associated with infectious diseases, medical breakthroughs have allowed us to live longer in the face of potentially dangerous conditions such as heart disease, cancer, and diabetes. However, in order to maintain the tremendous gains we have made, we must become partners in our own health and more actively participate in the choices that will impact it. The concept of living well is about how to take charge of our everyday life circumstances. Our own longevity is actually controlled each and every day by the decisions we make. Simple choices—from the food we eat to the exercise we get—can result in previously unsurpassed physical and emotional health.

There are some very promising developments taking place in mainstream allopathic (or traditional) medicine. Forward-thinking physicians like Arthur Agatston, MD, author of the best-selling book *The South Beach Diet*, and Michael F. Roizen, MD, and Mehmet C. Oz, MD, authors of *You: The Owner's Manual* and *You: Staying Young*, among other books, are providing us with information that allows for healthy lifestyle changes. The list of authors providing good and healthy information is long and distinguished. In addition to work being done by individual physicians, important research is underway at Harvard, University of Southern California, and my beloved University of Iowa, among other institutions of higher learning.

The march to better health is not being led by the medical community or pharmaceutical companies—it is being led by a growing number of cutting-edge physicians, researchers, and a throng of people just like you and me. I started my own journey to good health on the day I received the results of a mammogram that showed evidence of breast cancer. The diagnosis changed my life in ways that only those that are given such a medical diagnosis can fully understand. Today, I make life choices that will improve my odds of living longer and reduce my risk of fighting the cancer battle again. I am a cancer survivor but most importantly; I am a survivor. Later in this book you will learn about a supplement line I developed. Each and every ingredient in the line was selected as if my life depended upon the decisions I was making. I take the supplements everyday—and my life does depend on it. If I talk to you about a lifestyle choice in this book it is because I deeply believe that the advice may help you live longer and better.

My own interest in healthcare stems back to my work as a biochemist in the field of skin and wound care. I have been awarded two patents and invented six medical devices in the field. My Olivamine®-based skin care line is the leading brand sold into hospitals, nursing homes, home health and long-term care facilities. Tens-of-thousands of people use my products each month and I can assure you (and them) that when I formulated the products I did so with one thought in mind; to give them the best science I knew and to improve their quality of life. I currently have more than twenty skin-health products being sold around the world. The products are based on my proprietary blends of small molecules.

Taking care of our health is very personal—and our lives depend on getting it right. Equipped with strong interest and a belief that there has to be something better than what is being offered in the traditional disease focused medical arena, we are flocking to medical sites on the Internet and making physicians best-selling authors. It may take a decade or so, but good health care is coming. This new health care system will be based upon prevention using diet, exercise, and supplements as the foundation. If you do not yet believe that we must make changes, I point you to one very disconcerting World Health Organization (WHO) statistic: the United States spends more than any other nation on health care and yet we rank thirty-seventh in the world for quality of health care. But how do we rank in per capita costs?

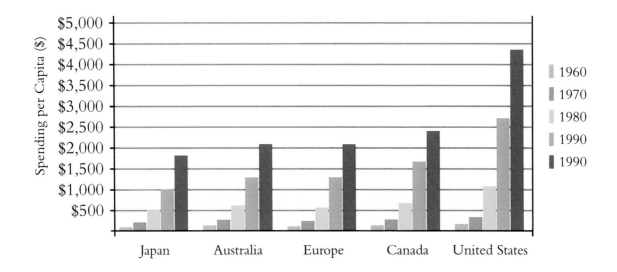

The health-spending chart tells the story about health care spending between 1960 and 1999. Spending increased from $144 per capita in 1960 to $4,400 in 1999, and it is expected to reach $7,500 per capita in 2008. We are spending a lot of money for our thirty-seventh place ranking! If you are a sports fan, you might suspect that the coach is about to be fired. The time has come for many of us to consider "firing" the system and to take over as coach of our own wellness team.

There are no outlandish or difficult aspects to this plan. The first step in developing a healthy lifestyle program is to recognize that it is a journey, not a race. If you try to make a lot of changes in your supplements, diet, exercise, and methods of relaxation, chances are good that you will fail. It is best to choose just a few changes at a time so that you will feel comfortable incorporating them into your daily life. It's about making simple choices. These choices should never be viewed as punishment, as most diet books imply, but rather they are a way to tend to your health while still enjoying all the good things in life: a glass of wine, a piece of chocolate, or a hearty laugh.

Throughout this book you will see references to "tuning up your engine." This analogy is simply meant to help you understand the importance of keeping your body "tuned" just as you would your car. If either your body or your automobile is left unattended, there will be breakdowns—and some could be major.

The proper functioning of the metabolic processes of our bodies keeps us running smoothly and helps us to be disease free, creating improved health and longevity. Most importantly, this "tune-up" can be achieved for very little cost and without prescription drugs—instead I suggest specific micronutrients including vitamins, minerals, and antioxidants. The optimum

intake of micronutrients varies between individuals and is based upon age and genetic makeup. In research conducted by Dr. Bruce N. Ames at the University of California, Berkeley, it was found that inadequate intake of folic acid and vitamins B_6 and B_{12} cause damage to DNA and the chromosomes in each cell; inadequate intake of zinc is related to further DNA damage. Dr. Ames found approximately fifty different human genetic diseases that can be corrected by higher doses of B vitamins.

As we age, the cells in our bodies need repair and this repair process requires that micronutrients be added to our diet. The addition of antioxidants, vitamins, minerals, and specialized micronutrients such as hydroxytyrosol, CoQ_{10}, acetyl-L-carnitine, and alpha-lipoic acid contribute to the metabolic "tune-ups" our bodies need to stay healthy. Just as with your car, giving your body the proper fuel and having regular checkups will contribute to long life.

Depending upon which study you read, we are taking in fewer than 40 to 80 percent of the micronutrients needed to maintain good health and metabolic efficiency. The micronutrients I am talking about are not some new potion. These are simply the essential vitamins, minerals, and other key micronutrients that our bodies rely upon to ensure good health and maximum life span. In other words, we are running on empty "metabolic" tanks and our "engines" are failing us—and the results of metabolic failure are heart disease, cancer, diabetes, and premature aging.

Let's be very clear here; for less money than you might spend on a special Starbucks coffee each morning, you can take a few supplements and thereby provide yourself with a marked increase in your body's ability to defend itself from diseases that reduce your life span and quality of life. Amazingly, millions of us choose the coffee!

Through simple lifestyle changes, you can improve your chances of living a disease-free life. If you already have experienced disease, these changes will improve your prognosis for the future. Billions of dollars are spent to treat ailments with prescription drugs rather than spending the pennies it would cost to instead prevent the disease. The better choice is a real life-and- money-saver—eat right, take supplements, exercise, and find ways to improve your mental and physical well-being.

And "one-a-day" vitamin supplements are not the answer. Taking such an approach is comparable to filling your car's tank with the cheapest fuel and not changing the oil. Just like your car, your body and its ten billion cells need a balanced supply of vitamins, minerals, antioxidants, and essential fatty acids to operate properly, and no single pill can provide these micronutrients. To properly tune your body's metabolic engine, you will need to take a multivitamin with antioxidants and key nutrients, an essential fatty acid (fish oil), and a mineral supplement. Unless you have additional special health needs, you can accomplish your micronutrient goals using just four products, along with added fiber (don't forget your fiber).

Before you implement any of the lifestyle changes outlined in this book, you need to know your current health status. The best way to learn the state of your health is to have comprehensive blood testing done—and be sure to get your own copy of the report. In the book, I provide you with my recommendations for the testing you should consider as part of your wellness plan. This is the critical first step in your journey to good health: You must know where you are today as you start your wellness journey. Once you know your blood test results you can develop a personal health plan that will get you fit and leave you "well tuned" as you progress along the path to a healthy life.

Today we can expect more than simply having one hundred candles on our birthday cake. We can have our cake and then celebrate the day with a great game of golf or an afternoon of tennis. The key to living well at one hundred™ is good planning. Come along on a journey to good health with our simple plan that will keep your body and mind healthy for years to come.

If I'd known I was going to live so long, I would have taken better care of myself.

—Leon Eldred

CHAPTER ONE
LONGEVITY

Wow! Living to 120!

Chapter 1: LONGEVITY

The number of people living past one hundred doubled between 1980 and 1990, and the U.S. Census Bureau projects that the number of centenarians will reach one hundred thirty-one thousand by the year 2010. The projections show a doubling every ten years, with the number reaching eight hundred thirty-four thousand by 2050. The growth in this population segment is so large that it is now called "Generation C" (the "C" here represents the Roman numeral for one hundred). Demographers are now counting the number of supercentenarians, defined as people age 110 or older.

In the past, it was an unusual feat when someone lived to what was considered to be the old age of seventy. Today, the fastest-growing population in the U.S. is people eighty-five or older. These days, with all our modern advances in medicine, treatment, and our healthier lifestyles, more and more people are living longer and enjoying their good health well into their golden years. *Scientific American* reports that there are currently more than sixty thousand people nationwide who are more than one hundred years old, up dramatically from just a decade ago. Many experts on aging say they are surprised every day by the number of people who are able to live without assistance well into their nineties. According to a group of scientists at Oxford University, the ability of people to live to the upper limits of 120 years of age will be possible due to advancements in modern medicine.

Life expectancy: the upward progression of this is interesting. When the Declaration of Independence was signed, life expectancy was just twenty-three years; in the 1800s, life expectancy was still under fifty years; in the 1900s we were expected to live into our seventies and eighties. Now it is predicted that anywhere from one to three million baby boomers will reach their one hundreth birthdays, while one in ten girls and one in twenty boys born today will live to be one hundred. Figures like these indicate that life expectancy is not set in stone. In fact, we have only scratched the surface of our understanding of the elements that impact it.

In past decades we were trained to believe that we were supposed to work hard, save for our retirement at sixty-five, live only a few years more, and then leave the rest of our accumulated money to family and friends. Now, with more baby boomers in this country reaching age one hundred, sixty-five may be considered middle-aged!

What do the Bible and the Internal Revenue Service (IRS) have in common? It may be hard to imagine, but both refer to the fact that you can live to 120. That's right! Genesis 6:3 states, "[Man's] days shall be a hundred and twenty years," while the IRS passed a ruling that went into effect on January 1, 2009, requiring that every actuarial table must anticipate that you may live to be 120. (I guess the IRS is just getting caught up on the two-thousand-year-old news.) Insurance companies, human resources departments, retirement fund planners,

financial institutions, and anyone else providing benefits to individuals over the course of their lifetimes use actuarial tables. These companies do not set the life expectancy criterion—your government (specifically, the IRS)—does. As a result, financial planners are spending trillions of dollars based on the belief that you are going to be living longer than ever before, well beyond one hundred. If you are sixty, according to your government, you are only middle-aged, and the phrase "the rest of your life" is taking on new meaning. We are clearly living longer than any of us ever imagined possible.

What does any of this have to do with you? Not only are prolonged life and good health great news for America's seniors from a lifestyle perspective, but they are also positive things from a life insurance perspective. Insurance companies will be adopting new actuarial tables that incorporate the new projected mortality levels within the next five or six years, many of them even sooner. Actuarial and mortality tables are utilized by life insurance companies to compute the probability of death by a certain age. In other words, they tell life insurance companies how long you are expected to live, on average, based on your age and sex. For the first time in more than twenty years, the American Academy of Actuaries has revised the tables to reflect America's trend toward living longer. The new tables increase the maximum (theoretical) life expectancy to 120 years, not because actuaries think many people will actually live to the age of 120, but because this is the absolute highest age that it is theoretically possible for a person to reach today.

According to the U.S. Centers for Disease Control and Prevention (CDC), in 2000, the average life expectancy for American males was seventy-four, up four years from 1980 (when the previous tables were written). For American females, the average life expectancy in 2000 was seventy-nine years, up two years from the 1980 tables. In addition, the annual improvement in male mortality of the general U.S. population has improved by 2 percent in the age group fifty-five to fifty-nine and has improved by 1.2 percent for females of the same age group.

Longer life spans mean that the mortality and expense charges you pay for insurance coverage should be lower, which should, in turn, lower your premiums: some insurance companies are claiming that the new tables will allow them to drop their rates by as much as 30 percent once they are adopted. Insurance companies benefit from the longer life spans of their consumers because they don't have to set aside as much money to cover death benefit payouts, so these savings should be passed on to their consumers.

(Some sources estimate that most insurance companies will be putting aside approximately 15 percent less than they currently do to cover death benefits. These changes mean that it is especially important to examine your insurance policy frequently and compare rates of various companies to see who has adopted the new tables and are therefore able to offer you lower rates.)

Your Genes and Aging

According to a geneticist at the Albert Einstein College of Medicine of Yeshiva University in New York City, your genes may have an important effect on how long you will live. If you have a relative who lived into his or her one hundreds, the odds are twenty times higher than those of the average person that you will live into old age as well. With that in mind, scientists are now working on figuring out how subtle differences in genes affect our longevity. Early studies have shown that there might be a link between insulin production and age-related diseases. A geriatrics specialist at the University of Hawaii found that an insulin-pathway gene in Japanese men over age ninety-five corresponded to improved energy usage. Another scientist noted that centenarians also have an improved amount of HDL (high-density lipoprotein), commonly referred to as "good" cholesterol.

With more centenarians and supercentenarians (those living past 110) being studied today, scientists are optimistic that target genes for longevity may be identified and studied. The New England Centenarian Study has already noted that there are even more similarities in genetic factors among supercentenarians than centenarians, thus perhaps making it possible to isolate those genes that may contribute to aging. Scientists have already determined that smoking, diet, and exercise affect whether we will live to our eighties in good health—with further research, we may be able to find other factors that lead to living well into our hundreds. But simply living longer, or increasing our life expectancy, does not address the key issue: It's not just about living long, it's about living well. This is no longer a matter of good luck—living a long and healthy life means maintaining good habits and becoming aware of the latest in genetic testing and scientific breakthroughs. Not only is it possible to just live to be one hundred it's possible to live a full and active life with many wonderful years to follow.

This discussion leads us to the basic question addressed in this book:

What Does it Take to Live a Long and Healthy Life?

Here are some factors:

- » Good genes
- » Healthy diet rich in fruit and vegetables
- » Exercise
- » Meditation and stress relief
- » Improved nutrition with supplements
- » Mental stimulation: for example, reading, classes, the visual arts
- » Socializing
- » Positive attitude
- » Reduced dependence on prescription drugs
- » Seeing a physician who prescribes changes in diet before prescribing drugs
- » Laughter
- » Music
- » Sleeping at least eight hours per night
- » Healthy lifestyle free of smoking and heavy drinking
- » Weight control

Our Answer to the Question is: All of the Above.

We are on a journey to good health and longevity. Small changes, or little steps along your journey to good health, will set you on a course that will allow you to be robust as you approach the century mark.

What Started the Longevity Revolution?

During the twentieth century, the ability to live longer was primarily the result of improved sanitation and the discovery of antibiotics. More recently, the many reasons for the improved journey to longevity can be attributed to technological advances never before possible. These advances have provided ways to treat or cure diseases, reverse aging, and repair damaged organs. Better diagnostic tools (including mammograms, MRIs, and other advanced tests) have contributed significantly to longevity. Medical science has developed treatments that boggle the mind—for example, the laparoscopic surgery techniques used to treat cardiovascular disease and perform other organ repairs are nothing short of amazing. The advances are even more astounding for those of us fortunate enough to be able to observe many of these new technologies while they are still on laboratory benches. Watching the enthusiasm of young scientists for the research they are doing and the scientific advances they are making provides me with an unparalleled belief in the ability to reach one hundred in good health.

However, along with scientific breakthroughs have come problems. The pharmaceutical industry has profited enormously by advertising and selling "miracle drugs" meant to cure every ill, and physicians are prescribing them at our expense. It is my goal to help you step back and take a closer look at the course that is being offered by pharmaceutical companies. And then offer a different journey toward good health, one that relies on your own personal ability to make small but important changes in your life.

You Are in Control

It is estimated that good genes—or the right genes, perhaps—account for just 25 percent of the longevity equation: that means that you control 75 percent of your destiny. Not only has technology pointed the way to living longer, but science has studied the ways in which our bodies react to small changes in lifestyle and attitude, setting you on a course that will allow you to be increasingly robust as you approach the century mark. In fact, researchers found that of those who crossed the one hundred-year mark, 75 percent of them were healthy enough to live at home and take care of themselves at age ninety-five. Researchers also have quantified the factors that lead to long, full lives. No longer do we have to simply guess about what is good for us and what is not. Specific changes in attitude and lifestyle have been proven to be effective in driving the forces that determine longevity.

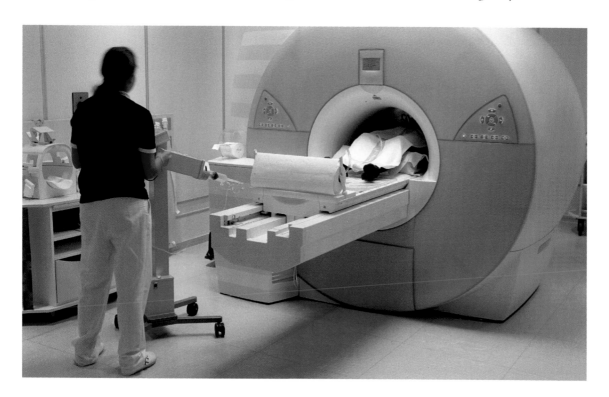

What Are the Leading Causes of Death Today?

While heart disease remains the number-one cause of death, the death rate for heart disease has steadily declined over the past fifty years, and the drop has been even more dramatic for stroke and other cerebrovascular diseases. Heart disease, cancer, and stroke together accounted for about seven of every ten deaths in 1980, but by 2005 that share dropped to five out of ten. The elderly are at particular risk for strokes, which is primarily caused by hypertension. Diabetes, Alzheimer's disease, and kidney disease—all of these commonly associated with aging—are still leading causes of death. The five leading causes of deaths from cancer in the U.S. are lung cancer (30.9 percent), followed by colon cancer (9.6 percent), breast cancer (8 percent), prostate cancer (6 percent), and pancreatic cancer (5.9 percent).

Leading Causes of Death in the U.S. (2005)

Disease of the heart	Heart attack (primarily)	652,091
Cerebrovascular disease	Stroke	143,579
Unintentional injuries	Accidents	117,809
Alzheimer's disease	Alzheimer's senility	71,599
Nephritis and nephrosis	Kidney infection	43,901

(Source: National Center for Health Statistics)

The top three causes of death in the United States are chronic conditions: cancer, heart disease, and stroke. More than 60 percent of all deaths of people sixty-five or older are a result of these major chronic conditions. According to the American Medical Association (AMA), these three conditions are often preventable: smoking, obesity, and alcohol consumption, in that order, all contribute to these causes of preventable death. The CDC report that 80 percent of older Americans are living with at least one chronic condition, and 50 percent have at least two: for example, chronic diabetes affects one in five Americans age sixty-five or older.

Older Americans are also getting fatter and have become more prone to bone and joint diseases such as osteoarthritis and rheumatism.

It has been shown that obesity, the second leading cause of preventable death, can now be controlled through diet, exercise, and medical technology. All it takes are simple changes in lifestyle to positively impact many diseases. What's more, not only does maintaining a healthy lifestyle add years to your life, it also allows you to spend those years without having to use a wheelchair or move into an assisted-living facility. While long-term health care is perhaps one of the greatest challenges we face in terms of spiraling health care costs, due to the major advances in what we know about how to protect our health, a turnaround is possible.

We can all take steps to curtail or alleviate our health problems just by making simple lifestyle changes that are available to everyone. It could be as easy as eliminating one slice of bread a day, going for a nice walk, taking a daily supplement, or meditating for a few minutes a day. In the meantime, scientists are developing new ways of repairing our bodies and prolonging life.

Can You Add Years to Your Life?

If you want to extend your life beyond the current expected lifespan of seventy years, there are numerous examples of ways to add years to your life by making simple changes in your lifestyle. In fact, there are many books on the market today that tell you how to add or subtract years from your lifespan by making a few basic changes.

One physician, Dr. Trisha Macnair, used hundreds of studies to quantify lifestyle changes that will contribute to extending your years. In her book *The Long Life Equation: 100 Factors that Can Add or Subtract Years from Your Life*, Dr. Macnair advocates simple changes in habits that can make a difference in life span. Dr. Michael Roizen used the same method in his book, The RealAge Makeover: *Take Years Off Your Looks and Add Them to Your Life*. According to these experts, it is important to note that these changes not only can affect how long you live, but also how well you live. Here are just a few of the steps you can take that can lead to more active years in your life:

Laugh more +1

Not only can laughter relax your whole body, but it also is a form of communication with others, an important factor in reducing anxiety and stress.

Stretch more +1

As we get older, we tend to be less active, which results in tight muscles and limbs.

Such conditions as arthritis and back or knee pain are a direct result of lack of suppleness. If you bend, stretch, and move, you will not only feel better, but you can also prevent injury and strain.

Eat breakfast daily +1

Eating a high-nutrient, high-fiber breakfast can jump start your day. It not only makes you feel better—those who eat breakfast can add one to three years to their life as opposed to those who skip breakfast.

Eat fiber +1

Fiber-rich diets can mitigate the risk of death from heart disease and cancer. While this perhaps seems to be a moderately difficult change for those of us who are not used to eating our recommended servings of fruits and vegetables, those portions are easy to get in a daily cup of blended fruit or vegetable juice.

Get a pet +2

Studies have found that animals can lower blood pressure and heart rates. A New York study concluded that heart attack survivors with pets were more likely to be alive one year later than those without pets.

Meditate +3

Those who meditate regularly say they have an increased sense of peace and tranquility. As it becomes more and more widely accepted, meditation has been shown to have measurable effects on lowering blood pressure and thus decreasing the risk of heart disease. It can even be more restful than sleep!

Increase balance +3

People over age sixty-five have a one in three chance of falling per year; these falls can lead to injuries such as broken hips or arms, or even fractured skulls or concussions. By participating in exercise such as tai chi or yoga, which involve muscle strengthening and balance training, such injuries can be avoided.

Keep an active mind +4

According to studies done by the Rush University Medical Center in Chicago, you can decrease your chances of getting Alzheimer's disease by nearly one half by doing activities that involve information processing, such as reading, going to museums, or doing crossword puzzles.

Get physically active +4

The Harvard Alumni Study of more than seventy-one thousand men found that burning 2,000 calories a week resulted in an increased life span of at least two years. Exercise works wonders on your physical and psychological health.

Brush and floss +6

Recent studies have linked periodontal disease to heart disease, diabetes, and respiratory disease. Healthy gums prevent bacteria from entering the bloodstream and thus causing serious problems.

Chapter 1 | Longevity | 16

The Living Well Proposition

In this book I will address many of the ways that you can lengthen your life, but most importantly, I will show you how you can have fun on this long-life journey. All you need is the willingness to take simple steps toward a long, happy, and vital life. It requires your belief that you can and should live well at one hundred™—and beyond. If it is a fact that we are living longer, then it is important for you to believe that you can make those years healthy ones. Living longer does not mean simply living disease-free: we also want to remain in control and stay vital. Science alone cannot save us from ourselves. We have to believe in our own ability to change. It may take focus and training, but it can result in an Olympian victory.

The extension of human longevity is one of our greatest achievements as humans, and amazingly, nearly half of the increase in life expectancy occurred during the twentieth century. We are now at a crossroads of sorts. In this promising new century, the time has come to give more consideration to how we each can take personal control of our health and set ourselves on a positive course. There are many choices to be made, and some of them can seem daunting. We want to trust the medical community, but more and more of us are turning to alternative and complementary medicine—and this is a good shift. Your attitude and active participation in your own health are giant steps forward in your personal journey to good health.

Even if you simply imagine what it might be like to be living well at one hundred©, you're on the right path. It's a wonderful journey: while it may take a little planning, if you come along with me you will not only live longer, you will live better.

TEN STEPS I AM TAKING ON MY JOURNEY TO GOOD HEALTH

Looked at my insurance policy to see if I am covered for the long-term

Learned more about living well at one hundred©

Planned my one hundreth birthday party

Looked at my lifestyle for ways to live better

Took an hour-long walk

Started a yoga class

Signed up for a class at the local junior college

Bought and started using dental floss

Added fiber to my diet

Checked to see if there were supercentenarians or centenarians in my town

Everyone who got to where they are had to begin where they were.

—Richard Paul Evans

WHERE ARE YOU NOW?

Start Your Engines!

Chapter 2: WHERE ARE YOU NOW?

What kind of longevity (health) plan do you have in place? Does it account for a long and healthy life? Does it anticipate that you will be playing golf or tennis on your one-hundredth birthday? Will you be playing with as much vigor as a younger player? We are not just looking to live a long life—we are looking forward to living well.

We are about to embark on a long and pleasurable journey to good health, but before we start, it's important to know where we are when we begin. We need to check the gas tank in order to know how far we can go. It's as if you were going on vacation—don't you want to make sure your car is ready to make the trip? If the "check engine" light is on, isn't it important to immediately take your car into the shop for repair?

Unfortunately, when it comes to something as important as our own health, we don't have a "check engine" light. We have to wait until engine failure before we are finally forced to deal with our own bodies. The most important journey of all—the one toward good health—is the one that we are the most unprepared to face. In order to begin your journey to longevity, you need to find a starting point; in order to determine your course, you need to get your engine checked. Every one of us has a different starting point. Unlike trained racecar drivers with perfectly tuned engines, we all have different conditions that may require specialized attention to get us started on our journey.

When you go to a repair shop to get your car checked, you may be given something like the 23-Point Vehicle Inspection. Are there any engine oil leaks? Do your tires have enough tread? Are your brakes in working condition? Is your air filter clean? Most vehicle repair shops give you a checklist before and after they look at your car. It serves as a diagnostic list and a service record.

We need a similar sort of checklist when we deal with our own bodies. Don't we all want to prevent health problems without having to spend our savings on surgery, hospitalizations, and other costly treatments? When I was doing the research for this book, I could not find

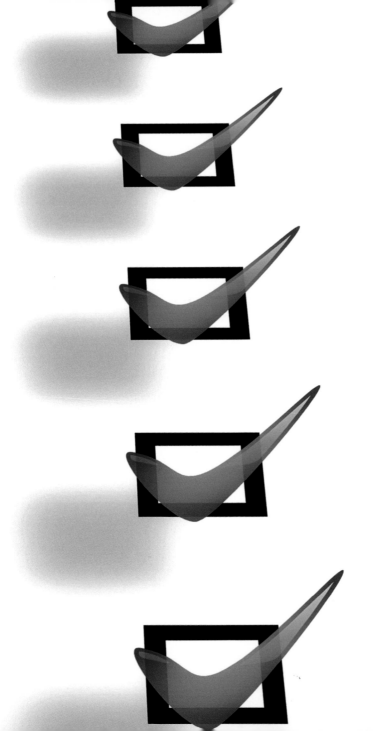

a comprehensive checklist anywhere, not even from a physician's office. It's easier to find a vehicle inspection list than to know what to check to maintain our own bodies! There are a number of tests to determine what can go wrong with your car, but how do you determine what could lead to a possible breakdown in your health?

For my book I've come up with a 23-Point Body Inspection list that's critical to have as we begin our journey to good health. This inspection begins with laboratory testing, including blood work and urinalysis, which is crucial to the maintenance of good health. The things that need constant monitoring—just as your brakes, radiator, tires, and drive belts do—are as follows:

- » Total cholesterol
- » Low-density lipoprotein (LDL) and LDL particles; small (critical) and large
- » Very low-density lipoprotein (VLDL)
- » High-density lipoprotein (HDL)
- » Triglycerides
- » Homocysteine
- » C-reactive protein
- » Glucose
- » Free testosterone/estradiol
- » Total testosterone/progesterone
- » Estradiol/DHEA
- » DHEA/free testosterone
- » PSA (prostate-specific antigen)/total testosterone
- » Liver function (AST, ALT, LDH, bilirubin, alkaline phosphatase)
- » Kidney function (creatinine, BUN, uric acid, BUN/creatinine ratio)
- » Immune cell counts (white cell count, lymphocytes, onocytes, eosinophils, basophils)
- » Red blood cell counts (hemoglobin, hematocrit, red blood cell count, MCV, MCH, MCHC, RDW)
- » Platelet count
- » Blood proteins (albumin, globulin, total protein, albumin/globulin ratio)
- » Blood minerals and vitamins (calcium, magnesium, vitamins A, B and D, CoQ_{10})
- » Macroscopic urinalysis (visual appearance)
- » Chemical urinalysis (pH, specific gravity, protein, glucose, ketones, nitrite, leukocyte)
- » Microscopic urinalysis (red blood cells, white blood cells, epithelial cells, crystals, cast, yeast, bacteria)

In addition to your basic blood test and urinalysis, it cannot be overemphasized that all of the following systems must be checked for possible diseases and for preventive and treatment purposes. These are examinations that need to be performed yearly and may require visits to several physicians.

System	Test
Cardiovascular	Basic physical, including stress test
	Cholesterol test
Cancer causes	Gynecologic exam
(prostate, breast, uterus, colon, etc.)	Prostate exam
	Mammogram
	Colonoscopy
Liver function	Basic physical
	Blood sugar test
Kidney function tests	Kidney function
Bone	Bone density scan
Skin	Dermatology exam
Vision	Eye exam
Hearing	Hearing exam

Laboratory Tests: What They Measure and What They Mean

When you go for your yearly physical examination, one of the first things a physician's office does is take a sample of blood for a blood panel. These laboratory tests check for markers for a variety of possible health conditions. The results of the blood panel are usually made available to you a few days after the examination, and it is important that you get a copy and keep it in your medical history organizer or folder. There will be variations in blood panel results due to many different factors, including diet, age, gender, physical activity, prescription drugs, alcohol intake, and a number of factors not necessarily related to illness. Thus, it is important to discuss the results with your physician so that you can learn more about your own body and possibly detect potential problems that may be overcome with small lifestyle changes.

There are many ways to spend your health dollars, but none is more important than comprehensive blood testing. I recommend blood testing should be done at least annually. To get the exact testing I recommend you go to my Web site at www.pinnaclife.com and click on the laboratory testing link. I have no affiliation with this company other than using (and paying) them for my own clinical trial work.

Thousands of people will suffer from diseases that were preventable through routine blood testing—indeed, some may die. Are you one of them? If you have not had a complete blood evaluation, there is that very possibility. In addition to having the testing done, it is important that you receive and keep a copy of the results of all lab work performed, especially your blood and urinalysis results. The laboratory report provides you with information about your results as they compare to "normal" ranges. If you see something that is out of range, you should make a note of the findings and speak to your physician. Some physicians redo the laboratory company's testing results report and put the results onto their own office's laboratory report forms. Ask your physician for the testing company's original document, not the physician's re-creation.

Simply taking supplements and improving your diet can correct most of the out-of-range findings. If there is a problem with one of your results, then do what is required to make the change if you can. For example, let's say the report finds you low in vitamin D (as most people are)—then you need to try to increase your time in the sun to ten to fifteen minutes a day (no sunscreen, please, because they block the production of vitamin D) and take a vitamin D supplement. Retest after six months and record your progress. This same process works for all nutritional results that are out of range.

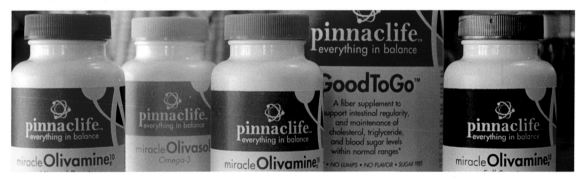

I recommend that you get a blood test as soon as possible and prior to starting your journey to good health. This way you have a starting point and then you can record your progress. Once you start your supplement program, retest in four months to check your progress. Of course, I recommend the Pinnaclife Supplements® as the pathway that will most likely get you on your journey to good health, but whatever you choose, make sure you are getting your vitamins, minerals, and essential fatty acids—what you need is to be on a well-balanced program.

If you only take one thing away from this book, let it be that you must have a complete blood testing if you want to know your health status. Let me repeat: you need to receive the results, and they need to be in your own personal health files. Take control of your health today and do not leave it in the hands of anyone else. If you are seeing a physician who does not think you need the testing or who feels that you should not have a copy of your test results, maybe it is time to move on and find another doctor. We all have the responsibility to ourselves to take charge of our health and do what is necessary to have a healthy life plan.

This book includes information about what your testing results may indicate, but I am not a physician—you must consult your doctor if you have a question. That being said, you must also do your own research. I had a physician tell me that my alkaline phosphatase levels were high, so he wanted to order more than $10,000 worth of additional testing. A second opinion provided me with the correct answer: my vitamin D levels were very low which created the high alkaline phosphatase reading. I took 2,000 International Units (IU) of vitamin D daily for several months, and my test results came into range. For less than $10, the problem was solved.

Personally, another test result that I take issue with is cholesterol. I believe that you should avoid statin drugs. I would make every possible nutritional, supplement, and lifestyle change possible before ever allowing a statin drug into your body. There have been entire books published on the dangers of statin drugs, most of them written by prominent physicians.

Someday we will look back on this class of prescription drugs and say, "What were they/ we thinking?" Try sustained-release niacin, a form of vitamin B, and see if your cholesterol numbers go down. Little by little, fiber, niacin, and phytosterols (or plant sterols) will help you chip away at high cholesterol without the side effect risks associated with statins.

Now is the time for you to take control. Get tested and be resolved to understand your results. You will become a much better patient, and your physician will appreciate that you want to discuss your results as you try to change your lifestyle to one of good health instead of illness.

Blood Panel Results

The results of a blood panel can help us measure the risks that predispose us to age-related diseases, but they are oftentimes difficult to interpret or understand. We should all have a basic understanding of what blood test results mean. Among the things that a blood test can measure are the following:

Total Cholesterol

Cholesterol is a fat-like substance in the blood that is associated with heart disease. In itself, cholesterol is not bad; in fact, our bodies need a certain amount of cholesterol to function properly. As the level of cholesterol increases, so does the possibility of artery blockage due to cholesterol plaque build-up, or atherosclerosis. When the arteries feeding the heart are blocked, a heart attack may occur. If the arteries that go to the brain are affected, the result is a stroke. The most critical number related to your health risks is your small LDL particle count (small LDL-P). You must know this number and you definitely want it to be low.

The three major types of cholesterol are high-density lipoprotein (HDL), low-density lipoprotein (LDL), and very low-density lipoprotein (VLDL). HDL cholesterol is considered "good" as it protects against heart disease by helping remove excess cholesterol deposited in the arteries. High levels may be associated with low incidence of coronary artery disease. LDL is considered "bad cholesterol" because cholesterol deposits form in the arteries when

LDL levels are high. The amount that is good for you may vary depending on other risk factors. VLDL is another carrier of fat in the body.

Triglycerides

Triglyceride is fat in the blood that is also associated with heart disease, as well as pancreatitis and other problems.

Homocysteine

This is an amino acid usually found in small amounts in the blood. Higher levels are associated with increased risk of heart attack. Levels may be high due to deficiency of folic acid or Vitamin B$_{12}$ associated with heredity, old age, kidney disease, or certain medications.

C-reactive protein

This is a marker for inflammation, especially in response to infection. It is also used to predict vascular disease, heart attack, and stroke. Inflammation is now considered, along with your small LDL-P results, the most important indicators of cardiovascular disease.

Glucose

This measures the amount of sugar in your blood. High values may be associated with eating before the test or diabetes. A fasting glucose is usually recommended to determine the normal range.

Estradiol/DHEA

This is a common type of estrogen and varies in women according to age and menstrual cycles; the level is affected by birth control pills or estrogen replacement.

Liver function (AST, ALT, LDH, bilirubin, alkaline phosphatase)

These numbers are a general index of overall health and nutrition. These are abbreviations for proteins—enzymes—that help cell chemical activity take place within cells. High values are associated with damage from alcohol, gallstones, damage to the bones and liver, and other diseases.

Kidney function (creatinine, BUN, uric acid, BUN/creatinine ratio)

Blood urea nitrogen (BUN), creatinine, and uric acid are waste products produced in the body. High values for these substances are indicators for decreased kidney function, as well as diseases such as gout and arthritis. BUN is also affected by high-protein diets, strenuous exercise, and pregnancy.

Immune cell counts (white cell count, lymphocytes, onocytes, eosinophils, basophils)

White blood count (WBC) is increased when infection occurs; it is also a marker for certain types of leukemia. Low WBC is a sign of bone marrow disease or an enlarged spleen, as well as HIV infection (in some cases).

Red blood cell counts (hemoglobin, hematocrit, red blood cell count, MCV, MCH, MCHC, RDW)

The hemoglobin is the amount of oxygen-carrying protein contained within the red blood cells. The hematocrit is the percentage of the blood volume occupied by red blood cells. Low levels suggest anemia, which can be due to nutritional deficiencies, blood loss, and destruction of blood cells internally, or failure to produce blood in the bone marrow. High amounts can occur due to lung disease, living at a high altitude, or excessive production of blood cells in the bone marrow.

Platelet count

This is the number of cells that prevent bleeding. High values can occur with bleeding, cigarette smoking, or excess production by the bone marrow. Low values can occur with acute blood loss, drug effects, and diseases such as leukemia.

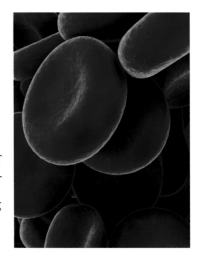

Blood proteins (albumin, globulin, total protein, albumin/globulin ratio)

Albumin and globulin measure the type and amount of protein found in the blood. They are a general index of overall health and nutrition. Globulin is important in fighting disease.

Blood minerals (calcium, potassium, phosphorus, sodium, chloride, iron)

The kidneys control your potassium level, which is important for the proper functioning of the nerves and muscles, particularly the heart, and readings can be affected if you are taking heart medication or diuretics (water pills). Any deviation from the so-called normal range should be monitored carefully. Sodium is also regulated by the kidneys and adrenal glands. Again, this test can be affected if you are taking diuretics or diabetes drugs, as well as by excessive water intake.

Blood vitamins (vitamins A, D, E and all of the B vitamins along with key nutrients)

Vitamins are an essential key to normal cellular function and health. Any deficiency in individual vitamins can give rise to disease and number of disorders. By having a vitamin analysis done you will know your body status with respect to several important vitamins and essential nutrients. The vitamin test profile measures Thiamin (B_1), Riboflavin (B_2), Niacin (B_{30}), Vitamin B_6, Folic Acid, Biotin (B_7), Vitamin B_{12}, Vitamin D, and Vitamin E). In addition key nutrients like CoQ_{10}, alpha-lipoic acid and carnitine (the only nutrient that you do not want on the high side of the range). If your carnitine level is high, you need to take carnitine because it is in your blood, and not in your cells, where it belongs.

Blood tests and urinalysis are the foundation of your health-testing program. But going back to our 23-Point Body Inspection list, you are just getting started. There are many more stops to make on your journey to good health and here are three that are important:

Vision Inspection

Our ability to participate fully in our daily activities is dependent upon our vision, and today we are learning more and more about the effects of aging on vision. More specifically, according to vision researcher Dr. Meredith Morgan, older adults experience five times more difficulty in activities involving visual search, peripheral vision, and cluttered visual scenes. More importantly, it has been noted that these conditions are rarely recognized by the people who suffer from them. It is all the more important that we get regular eye examinations by eye care specialists who are familiar with the specific vision problems that may occur among older adults.

Hearing Testing

An audiologist will perform your hearing test and should take the time to explain your test results. If you have any questions, or don't understand something, just ask. It is your hearing and you have a right to know. The results of your hearing tests will be recorded in a chart called an audiogram. An audiogram is a graph with red O's and blue X's connected with little lines. The O's represent the right ear and the X's indicate the left. Marks near the top of the graph are an indication of better hearing while marks further down the graph denote worse hearing. A 2004 MarkeTrak survey estimated that 31.5 million people reported hearing difficulty; that is around ten percent of the U.S. population. Three-in-ten people over age 60 have hearing loss; one-in-six baby boomers (ages 41-59), or 14.6 percent, have a hearing problem; one-in-fourteen Generation Xers (ages 29-40), or 7.4 percent, already have hearing loss. According to Richard W. Danielson, Ph.D. National Space Biomedical Research Institute and Baylor School of Medicine, Houston, Texas, noise is one of the most common causes of hearing loss in the United States.

Dental Care

Oral health is of critical importance in relation to aging, and there is a definite connection between periodontal health and overall health. Periodontal disease has been strongly linked to diabetes, as well as hypertension and cardiovascular disease. Along with drinking fluoridated water or using fluoride toothpaste, it is important to get regular dental checkups and brush and floss regularly. According to studies done at Emory University, people who

have periodontal disease have a 23 to 46 percent higher mortality rate than those with healthy mouths. Flossing is one of the easiest things you can do to stay young. Not only does it help protect your teeth against infection and minimize tooth loss, it can prevent and address much more serious systemic problems. In fact, bacteria found in plaque have also been found in fatty deposits that clog arteries.

How Well Are You Now?

This checklist may help in determining where you are now. Take the following test and see where you stand:

I'm a non-smoker	T	F
I exercise 3 to 4 days per week	T	F
I am not a diabetic	T	F
I get an annual checkup	T	F
I do not eat fast food very often	T	F
I eat two pieces of fresh fruit every day	T	F
My blood pressure is 120/80 mm/Hg or lower	T	F
My LDL cholesterol is 100 mg/dl or lower	T	F
My HDL cholesterol is at least 40 mg/dl	T	F
I am not overweight	T	F
I am generally happy with my job	T	F
I am in a happy relationship or I am happy being single	T	F
I generally don't drink more than 1 to 2 alcoholic drinks per day	T	F

If you answered true to most of these statements, then you are on the right road. If you answered "false" more often than "true," then don't wait another year to have a physical examination.

It's important to repeat that knowing your health starting point is as simple as doing a few things: Have your blood and urinalysis testing done and get a copy of the results from your doctor, get your vision and hearing checked, and see a dentist.

Are You Overweight?

Obesity is a major health risk so it is also important to chart your Body Mass Index (BMI). This is a self-evaluation to determine whether you are overweight, obese, or morbidly obese based on your height and weight. It is used to screen for health risks that may lead to medical problems. Just as it's good to know how much air is in your tires so you don't get a flat, it's important to know if we need to reduce our own body mass to avoid the risk of possible illness.

The following chart can be used to determine your BMI. To use the table, find your appropriate height on the left-hand column, then move across the row to your given weight. The number at the top of the column is your BMI.

If your BMI is 18.5 or less, you are underweight; a BMI of 18.5 to 24.9 is considered normal; 25.0 to 29.9 means you are overweight; 30.0 to 39.9 is considered obese; and 40 or greater indicates that you are considered to be morbidly obese. These determinations are important to note in terms of considering various options in your health care regimen.

Every health system is affected by obesity, so it is important to take a more critical look at your treatment options in determining how to deal with a BMI of 40 or greater. Obesity is on the rise in this country and now affects nearly one-third of the population. There is also an alarming rise in extreme obesity. This serious condition increases the risk of many health problems, including hypertension, osteoarthritis, high cholesterol, type 2 diabetes, stroke, heart disease, gallbladder disease, sleep apnea, and some forms of cancer.

HEIGHT	5'0"	5'1"	5'2"	5'3"	5'4"	5'5"	5'6"	5'7"	5'8"	5'9"	5'10"	5'11"	6'0"	6'1"	6'2"	6'3"	6'4"
WEIGHT																	
100	20	19	18	18	17	17	16	16	15	15	14	14	14	13	13	12	12
105	21	20	19	19	18	17	17	16	16	16	15	15	14	14	13	13	13
110	21	21	20	19	19	18	18	17	17	16	16	15	15	15	14	14	13
115	22	22	21	20	20	19	19	18	17	17	17	16	16	15	15	14	14
120	23	23	22	21	21	20	19	19	18	18	17	17	16	16	15	15	15
125	24	24	23	22	21	21	20	20	19	18	18	17	17	16	16	16	15
130	25	25	24	23	22	22	21	20	20	19	19	18	18	17	17	16	16
135	26	26	25	24	23	22	22	21	21	20	19	19	18	18	17	17	16
140	27	26	26	25	24	23	23	22	21	21	20	20	19	18	18	17	17
145	28	27	27	26	25	24	23	23	22	21	21	20	20	19	19	18	18
150	29	28	27	27	26	25	24	23	23	22	22	21	20	20	19	19	18
155	30	29	28	27	27	26	25	24	24	23	22	22	21	20	20	19	19
160	31	30	29	28	27	27	26	25	24	24	23	22	22	21	21	20	19
165	32	31	30	29	28	27	27	26	25	24	24	23	22	22	21	21	20
170	33	32	31	30	29	28	27	27	26	25	24	24	23	22	22	21	21
175	34	33	32	31	30	29	28	27	27	26	25	24	24	23	22	22	21
180	35	34	33	32	31	30	29	28	27	27	26	25	24	24	23	22	22
185	36	35	34	33	32	31	30	29	28	27	27	26	25	24	24	23	23
190	37	36	35	34	33	32	31	30	29	28	27	26	26	25	24	24	23
195	38	37	36	35	33	32	31	31	30	29	28	27	26	26	25	24	24
200	39	38	37	35	34	33	32	31	30	30	29	28	27	26	26	25	24
205	40	39	37	36	35	34	33	32	31	30	29	29	28	27	26	26	25
210	41	40	38	37	36	35	34	33	32	31	30	29	28	28	27	26	26

Obesity is a long-term disease that is extremely difficult to treat, but surgical options are now available. Perhaps you might want to consider the newest form of treatment utilizing lap-band technology, which has gained wide acceptance in the United States over the past ten years. Because of its overwhelming success, lap-band surgery has increased dramatically in the past two years. Completely reversible and adjustable, lap-band technology involves no cutting or stapling of the stomach. Approved by the U.S. Food and Drug Adminstration (FDA), gastric lap-band surgery is the least invasive form of weight loss surgery and involves gradual weight loss on a program that can be customized for each individual. If you are obese you are not alone and the medical option may help you get your health back. Lap-band is a medical breakthrough and I suggest that anyone with a BMI greater than 36 at least do some research on the Internet.

Keep Your Health Records

When it comes to dealing with wellness, it is important to keep and chart the results of all your tests. Are you charting your own health? We track our finances better than we do our own bodies. When it comes to our finances, we keep all of our receipts and records. We aggressively watch whether the stock market goes up or down, and we may even check on it on a monthly, daily, or even hourly basis.

One important thing we can do for ourselves is to get a notebook to track our health records. Get copies of all your blood tests and put them there; write down the doctors you have seen in the last year and when you saw them; record your prescriptions and note any changes in medication. You can even keep a journal of how you're feeling each day. Make it yours, and keep it in a safe place.

GLASBERGEN

Copyright © Randy Glasbergen.
www.glasbergen.com

"I try to eat healthy. I never sprinkle salt
on ice cream, I only eat decaffeinated
pizza and my beer is 100% fat-free."

You should use this form to write down as much information as possible about your blood testing, medical history, family history, and other crucial information so that you can refer to it the next time you have a medical problem. It may save your life!

Genetic Testing: Personalized Health Treatment

One of the most important and advanced technological tools that we have available to us today is genetic testing. From information gleaned with genetic testing, you can minimize the one-size-fits-all approach to medical treatment. Every body has twenty-three pairs of chromosomes that hold vital genetic information. DNA is made up of four chemical bases, and chromosomes are DNA molecules and associated proteins that carry portions of the hereditary information of an organism. Subunits of DNA are known as genes. Scientists scan a patient's DNA sample, which can be obtained from any tissue, for any type of mutation. There are currently more than four thousand diseases, including sickle cell anemia and cystic fibrosis, that are known to be genetic and are passed on in families. Alterations in our genes also play a role in such common conditions as heart disease, diabetes, and many types of cancer. We can now use genetic information not only to prevent hereditary diseases, but also to gain information about growing new cells that can be used to repair hearts or spinal cord nerves—all with our very own personalized genetic material.

With genetic testing, you can choose or avoid certain types of medications and treatments and follow a wellness plan that is devised specifically for you. The testing can also be used to determine the need for chemotherapy for cancer patients. My oncologist, Andrea Stebel, MD, recommended OncotypeDX testing (for breast cancer patients) to determine if I needed to go through chemotherapy. The outcome of the test determined that I was a very low risk patient. I was spared all the side effects of chemotherapy thanks to this caring physician that put me ahead of revenues derived from a treatment I did not need. Most important, I got to choose what was best for me based on good medical evidence, not on baseless fear.

Our advanced 23-Point Body Inspection includes a medical test that identifies changes in the twenty-three chromosomes. With a simple sample of saliva, blood, hair, skin, or other tissue, you can analyze your health parameters for every major disease. Genetic testing identifies changes in chromosomes, genes, and proteins. It is used to examine genes or markers near the genes. It is important to note that the results of this testing are different for every person because everyone's DNA is unique (including that of identical twins). I chose 23andMe® for my genetic testing. They may be a good choice for you.

In the near future you will no longer be treated with the same pill that is prescribed to treat thousands of people collectively, regardless of risk factors: instead, there will be a test that reveals specific information about your own individual genes; this information may be diagnostic and predictive of genetic variations that may increase the chance of developing a specific disease. Genetic testing is a sophisticated process that involves not only advanced laboratory procedures, but also accurate interpretation of the results.

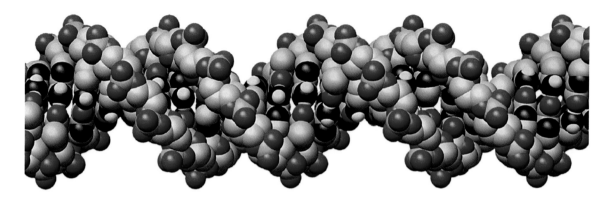

This interpretation may be difficult for those not specially trained in the field. The National Human Genome Research Institute (NHGRI) is a good source for up-to-date information on genetic testing. Much of the information currently available is the result of the work of the international scientific research project called the Human Genome Project (HGP), which was founded in 1990 to determine the makeup of the approximately twenty thousand to twenty-five thousand genes of the human body and to give scientists a map of that genetic information.

Genetic testing points to an important fact about our journey to good health: there's only one driver in this car, and that's you. Every car may not need the same tune-up, just as you can't rely on a single pill to fix everyone. The little pill you're taking may be wrong for you. (Consider this: more than fifty-five thousand people died from taking Vioxx, which was prescribed en masse to those with arthritis pain.)

Instead of focusing on disease once it has already done its damage, this type of testing emphasizes wellness, which is the positive direction we should all take with our health. Wouldn't it be helpful to detect potential diseases long before they actually occur? You have to refer to your own individual chart to determine what treatment is right for you. When it comes to our health, we are not exactly alike. That's why we need to examine and track our own individual checklists. I emphasize again that it is crucial to know where you are when you start so that you can then begin your journey, one small step at a time.

TEN STEPS I AM TAKING ON MY JOURNEY TO GOOD HEALTH

Got a blood test

Wrote down the date of my last checkup

Made a "Health Organizer" to keep all my health records in one safe place

Determined my Body Mass Index

Made an appointment for a colonoscopy

Wrote down a family history of health problems

Looked on the Internet to find out who does genetic testing in my area

Checked with my insurance company to see if they cover genetic testing

Made a list of all my prescriptions and their side effects

Relaxed with a glass of wine

For every failure, there's an alternative course of action. You just have to find it. When you come to a roadblock, take a detour.

—Mary Kay Ash

CHAPTER THREE
HEALTH

Say Goodbye to the Pharmaceuticals!

Chapter 3: HEALTH CARE

Have you ever planned a vacation only to have things not work out as you'd intended? In our journey to good health, we all got on a train built and run by pharmaceutical companies—this train was supposed to take us to destinations such as "better health," "cure," and "well-being." While we may have gotten close to some of these places, we never arrived. It's time to change our travel agent and take a new direction.

What you are going to read in the next few pages may seem negative. It is hard to present the pertinent information in this chapter and give it a favorable spin. However, in order to move forward we need to take a close look at where we are today and examine why it is not a very good place to be. We will look back at this part of our journey and examine how and why we have gotten into this mess.

Some may say that the focus on profits rather than patient care became an addiction for many in the pharmaceutical industry. Like the ill wind of a tornado, this wrong emphasis twisted physicians and patients alike in the storm's destructive path. I am going to call your attention to what has happened to millions of Americans caught in this health care storm.

It has taken us almost three decades to get to this part of our journey; we are here, in part, because most of us were raised to put our trust in health care providers. As we travel in our cars on vacation, we may find that there are long stretches of road that are desolate, but we know that we will reach the perfect location that we have been dreaming about at the other end. Regarding health care, we may look back at our journey to better health and see some parts as desolate. We have been in health care desolation, and we are just now emerging on the other side.

Over the next decade the health care journey promises to be a very exciting trip. We will go from impersonal medicine—one pill fits all—to personalized health care where each treatment is designed just for us. Let's look back from where we are right now so that we can see what went wrong; by doing this we can have hope for our future.

According to Dr. Gary Null's book, *Death by Medicine*, one hundred and six thousand Americans died in 2003 from complications of/or reactions to prescription drugs, but the actual number of deaths is estimated to be two to four times that number. Millions of us seek to cure our problems by taking a prescribed pill. When we pick up our prescriptions they always come with a sheet of paper that gives extensive warnings about possible side effects. The lure of the quick fixes often causes otherwise bright people to begin a treatment course that may result in health complications or even loss of life.

The ride we are currently on has been caused by a pharmaceutical industry that has lost its moral and scientific compass. What started out sixty to seventy years ago as an industry working to create extraordinary cures for diseases

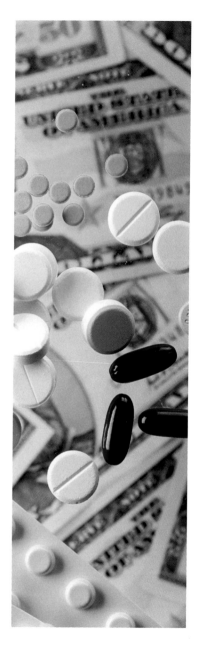

such as polio and tuberculosis has evolved into the business of creating prescription drugs: these drugs are the leading cause of death in America. Every five minutes, twenty-four hours a day, one of us will die from taking prescription drugs as directed. Most of us would never consider taking dangerous and addictive so-called street drugs. However, millions of us take prescribed drugs—these are dangerous and addictive as well. As a society, we have gone from taking an average of seven prescriptions a year in 1993 to an average of twelve per person in 2000. According to a Kaiser Family Foundation report, U.S. spending for prescription drugs in 2006 was more than five times the amount spent in 1990. The spending number is predicted to soar to $414 billion by the year 2011.

The evidence is overwhelming that the review process for approval of new medications has become lax. The FDA now accepts huge sums of money, called "user fees," from the pharmaceutical companies to pay for the costs associated with moving their proposed drugs quickly through the approval process. Once these drugs are "fast-tracked" by the FDA, physicians who may be financially linked to the pharmaceutical company are often approving these new drugs. Talk about the fox in the henhouse! This is what I mean when I say the pharmaceutical industry has lost its moral compass.

Let's look at a specific case in point: Vioxx. Vioxx is a drug that was given rapid priority by the FDA. When it became evident that Vioxx caused heart attacks—and after

Dr. David Graham of the FDA reported to Congress that fifty-five thousand people had died as a result of taking the drug—it was discovered that the physicians on the panel that approved the drug and kept it on the market had direct ties to the pharmaceutical company that made and sold Vioxx. Moreover, information has recently been released to support the claim that a 1999 clinical study of Vioxx was done only to support a marketing plan prior to the drug's launch, exposing that study's participants to potentially dangerous side effects solely for the intended purpose of mass marketing. A huge marketing budget was then used to keep the drug in the marketplace (selling it to you and me) and to slow the FDA recall process. Together the FDA and pharmaceutical industry allowed thousands of unnecessary deaths until finally, reluctantly, they removed the product from the market.

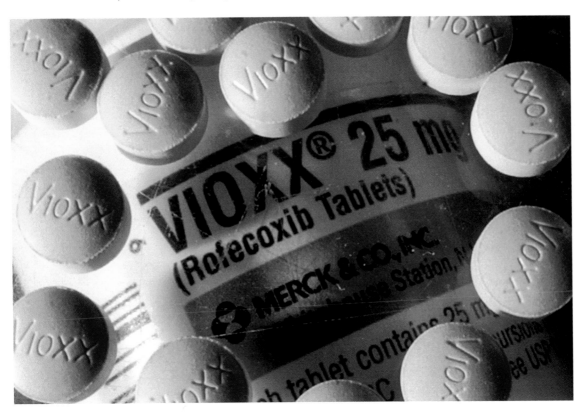

So let's review: a pharmaceutical company that failed to do the "real" scientific study nevertheless got their drug on an FDA "fast track." This drug was approved for use by a panel of physicians who had the opportunity to benefit from proceeds of the product's sales. When the "real" clinical study was done—the one in which unsuspecting patients were given the drug and subsequently died—the pharmaceutical company and the FDA panel did everything possible to keep the drug on the market because it was so profitable. Only when more than fifty thousand people died did the FDA reluctantly remove it from the market.

There is an advertisement running on television right now with this tag line: "Your pharmaceutical companies want to help." Every time it appears on the screen I want to know why the pharmaceutical companies that "want to help" don't have to tell the viewers about those people who have died needlessly after using their products. Let's stop this trip and instead take a new direction. There's very little difference today between an advertisement for the latest drug and a commercial for a new car. Even though the ads may look the same, the effects are far different. The only dangers in buying an advertised car is that you may not get the best deal from the dealership, it may not get the promised gas mileage, or you may not be able to buy it at all—these are not life-threatening situations. However, there is a risk of serious illness, even death, if you are persuaded by the pharmaceutical advertisement. Pharmaceutical companies' television advertising exaggerates their products' benefits. They use happy, smiling actors who seem to be having a wonderful life or feature celebrities such as Sally Field who apparently are using the drug; these ads meanwhile minimize the risks of the drugs being promoted. Such advertising is paying off for the drug companies: surveys indicate that when a patient goes into their physician's office, they are looking for a specific, brand-name drug rather than a generic one. Seventy percent of these patients are then prescribed that exact drug, the one they saw advertised on TV.

It was reported in the *Annals of Family Medicine* (Frosch et. al., 2007) that you will watch between fourteen and twenty hours of television commercials produced by pharmaceutical companies this year. These companies will spend nearly $5 billion trying to make you think that you may have some illness that requires treatment with one of their pills. This kind of direct-to-consumer advertising is allowed only in the United States and New Zealand. What's more, the amount spent on advertising by pharmaceutical companies is up from the $2 million they spent to get your attention in 1980. As a result, we are paying more than ever before for prescription drugs.

How can an industry get away with this? It's simple: we want to trust the drug companies, and we want to trust our physician to prescribe the drugs that we think we need. Every day and night pharmaceutical companies come into our homes with expensive advertisements created by the most high-powered advertising agencies in the world. The task of these advertising agencies is simple: to make you believe that you have a health problem or to make you think that a "miracle" cure is possible if you just take a magic pill. At the end of these commercials, at a verbal word rate heretofore saved for auctioneers, the voiceover starts spewing out all of the drug's side effects. What does this battle over your health, the struggle between the pharmaceutical and wellness industries, have to do with living well at hundred[©]? I am positive that if you take unsafe prescription drugs or too many prescriptions, you are not going to make it to your one-hundredth birthday party.

"With this new drug, cholesterol forms *outside* of the body, where it can't clog the arteries."

If you take the information provided in a drug advertisement to your physician and tell him or her that you think the "magic pill" you've seen described will cure the problems you have experienced, my guess is that you will most likely get what you asked for; in part, this is because, in the few minutes physicians have to spend with each patient, there is generally not enough time for them to argue. We trust our highly educated physicians to give us something we will need in order to help us recover or even survive. Even those "samples" that the physician gives you in the office eventually cost you in the long run. Doctors usually end up giving out samples of costly name-brand drugs or prescribing them over less-expensive generic ones. There's never been such a thing as a free lunch, and there is certainly no such thing as a free "drug" lunch.

So are you actually getting that miracle pill you asked your doctor for, or are you getting a sugar pill? In a study reported in October 2008 in the *British Medical Journal* and conducted by the U.S. National Institutes of Health (NIH) in which American internists and rheumatologists were surveyed, it was found that half of American doctors regularly give their patients placebo pills without telling them. This behavior is in stark contrast to the advice from the AMA that recommends that "doctors only use treatments to which patients have given their informed consent."

The following comments are found in the published study: "It seems like doctors are doing things they shouldn't be doing," said Dr. Irving Kirsch, a professor of psychology at

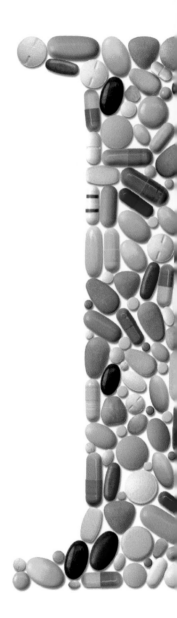

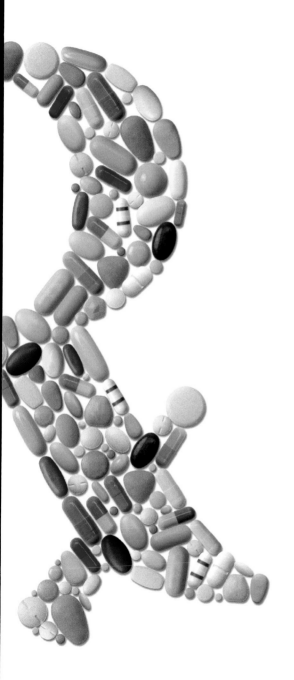

the University of Hull, who has studied the use of placebos but who was not linked to the published research. "Doctors may be under a lot of pressure to help their patients, but this is not an acceptable shortcut."

Half of the doctors in the study reported using placebos several times a month. Nearly 70 percent of those who did so described the treatment to their patients as "a potentially beneficial medicine not typically used for your condition." Only 5 percent of doctors explicitly called it a placebo treatment. In the survey conducted by the NIH, doctors were asked if they would recommend a sugar pill for patients with chronic pain if it had been shown to be more effective than no treatment—and nearly 60 percent of doctors said they would.

Here's a question: If half of the medicine being prescribed is dangerous and has side effects beyond its value, and the other half of the "prescribed" pills are sugar, then why are we continuing to support the current medical system? Who really cares about you? The answer should be, "You"—it is time for you to take your health care seriously.

When a physician writes you a prescription, there's something else they may not be telling you: each prescription you fill at the local pharmacy is tracked (except for those sugar pills discussed above) by the pharmaceutical industry, and some physicians who prescribe heavily are richly rewarded. These rewards go far beyond expensive lunches and dinners. Ninety percent of all continuing medical education (CME) classes for physicians are given and paid for by pharmaceutical companies—and lavish trips to Vail or cruises to exotic places create the perfect classrooms for lessons on how to overprescribe. In order to remain certified, physicians must prove they have taken part in continuing medical education. That's a good idea, but not when 90 percent of the CME materials are produced by the pharmaceutical companies.

Pharmaceutical companies are spending on average $8,000 to $15,000 per year per physician. No wonder brand-name drugs cost so much money. Perhaps the prescription drugs available from Canada are cheap not because they are of lesser quality, but because the elaborate payoff system is not in place. The pharmaceutical companies also employ more than one hundred thousand company representatives, called "detailers," who call on physicians in the U.S., and they spend $12-15 billion a year to promote themselves to physicians.

Pharmaceutical companies do not stop at our physician's doorstep. Every major nonprofit health organization, from the American Cancer Society to the American Heart Association and everything in between, takes money from pharmaceutical companies. Although these organizations are charged with providing us with independent information, they are not doing so because, simply put, they need the money. The pharmaceutical industry infestation into these organizations has turned them into "cheerleaders" for that industry.

I would like to point out a difference between the American Heart Association and the American Cancer Society. The American Heart Association has embraced the importance of emphasizing changes to an individual's lifestyle, including better nutrition and supplements. The American Cancer Society, on the other hand, cannot even recommend vitamin D_3 for breast cancer patients despite overwhelming scientific evidence of its effectiveness. As a scientist and a breast cancer survivor, I cannot support them even though I recognize that thousands of well-intended people have worked long and hard for the stated goal of "finding a cure." I have worn the pink ribbon pin, contributed, and walked for their cause—but no more!

How much is this trip to Pharmaceutical Land costing us? In 2004, American Association of Retired Persons (AARP) surveyed prescription drug pricing and discovered that prices have been escalating at three times the rate of inflation. Increased drug prices come at a time when the cost of almost everything we use has come down, for example, the costs of our computers, big-screen TVs, cell phones, etc. Not so with pharmaceutical pricing—and now you know why.

The best way I have found to protect yourself from the rising costs of prescription drugs is to buy your medications from Costco. You can look up costs on their Web site www.costco.com and go to the "Drug Pricing" link. When most pharmacists ask you if you want to buy a generic brand and save, they do not tell you that what is really happening is that they are making more money. You may save 10-20 percent by selecting the generic brand but that generic brand may cost the pharmacy 1,000 percent less. Let's look at just a few examples of savings I found on the Costco site recently. Costco is different in that they pass the savings on to you and for that they deserve our business. The chart to the right gives you the price you would pay Costco if you

Brand vs. Generic Pricing

Zocor 10mg Tablet (MSD) 50 count		$137.11
Generic Alternative/Simvastatin		$9.93
Zocor 20mg Tablet (MSD) 50 count		$237.17
Generic Alternative/Simvastatin		$7.21
Zoloft 100mg Tablet (ROE) 60 count		$212.84
Generic Alternative/Sertraline HCL		$16.60
Prozac 10mg Puvule (DIS) 56 count		$276.24
Generic Alternative/Fluoxetine		
HCL Capsule (SAN)		$7.41
Prozac 20mg Pulvule (DIS) 56 count		$288.03
Generic Alternative/Fluoxetine		
HCL Capsule (SAN)		$7.31

Source: costco.com

insisted on the "brand" name and the price they offer you if you allow them to provide you with the "generic alternative." The list goes on and on but you get the idea. We have to be smart about our prescription purchases. The more we demand the pharmacies to charge us fairly for our prescriptions, the more the entire industry will become accountable.

What's Making Medical News?

I thought that I would do a little test. Today, October 22, 2008, I looked for articles in the *Wall Street Journal* and *USA Today* for information about drug companies and health-related issues that may be of interest to you. I found three articles, two in the *Wall Street Journal* and one in *USA Today*. The point here is not that I found the articles—the question is, did you find them? Are you looking for articles about how the FDA, pharmaceutical companies, and the medical community are conducting themselves? This information is there for you, and you should pay very close attention, because being an informed health consumer may save your life.

In the *Wall Street Journal* article titled "FDA Is Faulted for Oversight of Foreign Drugs," I learned that the FDA inspects U.S. pharmaceutical manufacturing companies about every 2.7 years. While this is clearly not often enough, they only inspect foreign pharmaceutical manufacturing facilities—including those in China—about every thirteen years. This is not a typographical error! Is it any wonder Americans are dying from the prescription medicines we take? Is the pharmaceutical industry, with the FDA's help, getting away with risky behavior? Think about this and come to your own conclusion . . . it may save your life. Remember, I want to you get you to your hundredth birthday!

The headline of the second article in the *Wall Street Journal* read "Lilly [Eli Lilly and Company] Nears Settlement in U.S. Zyprexa Probe." The article informs the reader that Eli Lilly has set aside $1.42 billion to settle charges that it downplayed side effects of its drug Zyprexa (used to treat schizophrenic and bipolar disorders). This is in addition to the settlement of nearly sixteen hundred product liability lawsuits; resulting in payments of $62 million to states and the District of Columbia settling consumer protection claims.

Now for the *USA Today* article, "'On the Market' Doesn't Mean a Drug Is Safe." The article states, "One-in-four recently approved biological products needed some type of regulatory action." The problem is that these regulatory actions came between 3.5 and 5 years after the products were launched, and thousands of us paid the price. Catherine DeAngelis, editor, and Phil Fontanarosa, deputy editor, of the *Journal of the American Medical Association* (JAMA) reported the findings. Here are their comments: "The human body is in a constant state of change, and the effects of some drugs will manifest only after exposure over time." They further state "many post-market studies manufacturers agree to as a condition of FDA approval are either never completed or not completed in a timely manner."

Three Additional Days of Medical News That You Should Think About

It is crucial to really watch and read the medical news that may save your life. Within a few days, in early November 2008, there were several additional articles related to heart disease.

November 9, 2008: The *Washington Post* presented the findings of a study on the use of statins by people with normal cholesterol levels to reduce the risk of heart attack and stroke. AstraZeneca—the maker of Crestor, one of the leading statin drugs—funded the "unbiased" study. Study authors predicted that Crestor, based upon the study results, would be a new "blockbuster" drug.

November 10, 2008: *USA Today* reported on studies that put a price tag on the use of statin drugs such as Crestor if their use was expanded and used to reduce cardiovascular disease. The cost of saving lives with Crestor, for patients at risk of cardiovascular disease who did not have elevated cholesterol, would be $557,000 per person. This would represent an increase of $10 billion per year in the nation's medical bill—good news for AstraZeneca, but not for the country.

November 11, 2008: *U.S. News and World Report* presented study results that demonstrated that the following six lifestyle changes reduced the risk of cardiovascular disease for just pennies and without all of the side effects associated with Crestor:

Stop smoking	Eat olive oil, fish, and nuts
Get active	Shrink your waist size
Get enough sleep	Reduce stress

These articles reinforce the fact that you must look out for yourself. Do not take any prescription drug on blind faith. If it is new on the market, there is a one-in-four chance the drug may be recalled or reformulated because of very serious side effects. As in the case of Vioxx, the side effects may be fatal. Pay attention as though your life depended upon it—because it does.

As a society and a country, we can no longer trust the recommendations of pharmaceutical companies when they are funding and promoting the very studies that would increase their profits by billions of dollars each year. Instead, trust your good judgment and watch the news for alternative information like the examples above: in just three days we went from Crestor being the new "blockbuster" drug to recommendations that we follow the commonsense approach of healthy lifestyle choices.

The pharmaceutical industry has penetrated our lives over the past few decades. They always seem to have the "magic pill." But do their advertising claims really add up? Let's look at the example of medications to treat heart disease: despite all of the prescription drugs we have been convinced would save our lives, between 1980 and 2006 the number of people hospitalized for heart failure increased 131 percent. The study findings on this increase were reported in the *Washington Post* on November 9, 2008, the very day they published the story about Crestor being the new "blockbuster" drug. You need to choose a path to natural health not the pharmacy way that may shorten your life!

I cannot fail to mention here that the industry we are talking about is the same industry that tells you that supplements, made right here in the U.S. (not in a foreign country), are not safe! In fact, supplement-manufacturing companies are inspected more often and regulated more closely than pharmaceutical companies. By now you may have sensed my not-so-veiled mistrust of the pharmaceutical industry. In my opinion, since the 1960s the pharmaceutical companies have "drugged" us into believing that they were helping us achieve a long and healthy life. This is simply not true. Greed, false reporting, and a host of other acts on the part of the pharmaceutical industry have led us to become, as author Greg Critser terms us, "Generation Rx." I, for one, do not want any part of this, and I believe that we should all try to redefine ourselves: We can become part of the healthiest generations of all time. The time has come to flush what is bad for us and embrace what is good. This is the ultimate lifestyle change.

The Shift to the Science of Prevention

There is a major change taking place in health care due to the realization that treating disease is not working. This is good news, and it will affect your life right now as well as your ability to live a happy, healthy life for many years to come. The key to this shift is prevention. Instead of treating disease, today health care professionals are using diagnosis and new technologies for early detection rather than prescribing drugs.

We are swiftly moving from the treatment of disease to the prevention of disease. At the Emory Center for Health Discovery and Well Being (part of the Emory/Georgia Tech Predictive Health Institute), this switch has been put into action. In a program that custom-designs health care based on an individual's unique characteristics, biological factors that predict disease are being identified, thus enabling prevention methods to be applied to those specific indicators. Tests are conducted to determine four basic processes in the human body: inflammation, immune function, use of oxygen, and capacity to regenerate blood stem cells. For example, testing for C-reactive protein can measure the amount of protein in the blood that signals acute inflammation; this process needs to be regulated to guard against damage to healthy tissue. A test for oxidative status can determine if fuel is being used efficiently to convert oxygen to energy. Just like your car, your body can misfire, which in turn causes fuel to be used inefficiently and produce harmful waste products known as free radicals. Studies have shown that free radicals are associated with certain cancers, as well as hardening of the arteries.

Tests such as those being conducted at Emory are extremely helpful in identifying a disease condition before it happens, and this work is now being shared with researchers from Ohio State University, Vanderbilt University, Duke University, and others in order to open the

door to predictive health and personalized medicine and to shut the door on the pharmaceutical industry's focus on treating disease.

We live in a time where ordinary citizens are increasingly choosing to make lifestyle changes rather than taking prescription drugs. This shift is not a trickle—it is a flood. From buying organic foods (First Lady Michelle Obama has planted an organic garden at the White House) to cutting back on fat intake, we are all trying to be just a little healthier. Millions of us now take supplements every day to ensure that we are getting necessary nutrients. We are turning en masse from prescription drugs to healthy medicine such as supplements, good nutrition, and engaging in a belly laugh; instead of popping a pill, we are popping a comedy DVD into the player and spending a couple of hours simply laughing our way to happiness. Good for us! If you have made any of these changes, no matter how small, congratulate yourself. You are on the path to good health, and the journey will be rewarding.

WHERE DO WE GO FROM HERE?

There is more good news ahead as we take on the pharmaceutical industry. Prominent medical school professors are now joining in asking for a prohibition of direct-to-consumer marketing of drugs. The reason for this is simple: drugs can cause harm, and patients are often misled into making their own prescription decisions by insisting on a certain drug they saw advertised. Remember, you will only see these drug company commercials in the United States and New Zealand. They are illegal everywhere else.

With the patents on many of the top drugs set to expire after twenty years on the market, we are soon going to see more generic drugs being sold. Such generics are typically available at lower prices, as opposed to the 90 percent profit margin on such patent-protected drugs as Lipitor, Zocor, Fosamax, and Singulair. The chairman of pharmaceutical giant Eli Lilly and Company has expressed dismay over the future of the industry after these major patents expire. Because no new drugs have appeared on the horizon to take the place of the major moneymaking drugs, many in the pharmaceutical industry are discussing a shift to biotechnology, where laws currently do not allow the development of generic drugs.

Another major advancement on the horizon is the effort to use genetic testing to determine which prescription drugs will work for you. Such testing might ensure proper dosages as well as possible alternatives to treatment if used in conjunction with the patient's specific genetic profile. A study is currently being conducted in conjunction with the FDA to develop such profile studies. Right now, we have a one-pill-fits–all mentality, but we're going to go rather quickly from that one pill that serves millions to an individualized plan based on the individual makeup of your own genes. Our genes have a code, a language with messages that we're just beginning to learn. As we learn the language of each patient's genes, we're going to make slight changes to how individuals are treated. In the next decade, medicine is going to go from mass-produced treatment to individualized medicine.

We have gotten ourselves in this situation with the pharmaceutical industry over the last thirty years. We made decisions to take drugs because we thought they had great promise. And although many prescription drugs have helped, they have also hurt. The time has come for us to take responsibility for our own health and to seek personalized medical care. You may have higher cholesterol than I do, but your high cholesterol may be quite normal for you while my low cholesterol may not be good for me. If your high cholesterol is not causing cardiovascular disease, why should we treat it?

This is an exciting new way of looking at medicine. You can now take a test that detects the overall functioning of the arteries to determine your risk for heart disease. You can also take a test for oxidative stress to check for the risk of free radicals. All of these tests are meant to check how your body, and yours alone, is processing potential markers for disease.

What's even more exciting is what's in store for you in the future in terms of genetic testing. You can take a simple test—a saliva sample on a swab—the lab results will indicate a treatment plan just for you. The cost of a DNA test, which would have been tens-of-thousands of dollars a few years ago, can be as low as $400 today; genetic testing is going to be as routine in three to five years as blood testing is today, and this will move us toward personalized medicine that focuses on prevention, not disease. Some insurance companies cover testing done for a specific purpose, but you should not count on being covered just yet.

Some genetic testing is now available for as little as $100. This type of testing reveals how a particular medicine will or will not work for us individually: a medicine that may cure you may not help me at all. Within a very short period of time it will be unthinkable to take a medicine without knowing how it will affect you. Before you submit to chemotherapy associated with breast cancer, for example, an OncotypeDX test will let you know if the chemotherapy will help you. These are not tests that are still on the drawing board: they're here now.

Even more amazing is the field of bioinformatics, which involves the development of data processing and storage through computer technology. Microsoft estimates that fifty thousand people worldwide are now working in this field. Not only will information be available at your physician's fingertips, but also your own medical history may be tracked more quickly and completely than ever before.

WHAT CAN WE DO FOR OURSELVES?

Don't Be Afraid to Know

People sometimes don't want to undergo genetic screening because they are afraid they will find out that they're predisposed to a medical condition. Remember, you are predisposed, and this predisposition is already written in your genetic code. Address problems early on: not knowing about something is not going to make it go away. Knowledge means you can do something about it—ignorance is not the answer. The rejection of genetic testing can be likened to our fear of technology: In this rapidly changing world, everything new is a little scary; while it may be scary, the technology coming in medicine is going to save our lives, and we need to find a way to embrace it. It's part of a journey, and not an optional one. Newness gives us pause, and that's okay, but your willingness to embrace genetic testing will reduce your risk of disease as long as you have a personalized wellness plan.

We have to stop focusing on illness and focus on wellness. New terms that address this shifting attitude have been coined: we now refer to the "wellderly" and the "illderly." The people with a wellderly way of life will enjoy a long and pleasurable existence, while those who define themselves by their health problems may become part of the illderly generation. We must all develop the habit of wellness.

Track Your Journey Away from Prescription Drugs

You don't have to make a complete change from taking prescriptions to taking no drugs; you may not even get off half of your prescriptions. This is not the Boston Tea Party where you throw all your pills into the harbor! But every single medication you can take off your prescription list is a step in the right direction: if you're taking five medications, maybe you can reduce that to two, or you may be able to go from taking 50mg to 10mg. Every reduction in the number of prescription drugs you take is a milestone.

You can start this journey with the following plan: Make a chart of all the medications you are taking, including the dosage and what it is intended to treat. Be sure to list the possible side effects, and be honest with yourself about what each side effect may mean to your health. You must ask yourself: Is taking this drug worth these risks? Once you make this list, ask yourself, can the dosage be reduced or the medication stopped? Then, take your thoughts to your physician and have a talk. Don't make any changes in your medications without his or her input.

Choose Your Physician Wisely

In the new world order there is going to be a major shift in health care. The role of the physician will dramatically change. Today, the physician is a primary care provider, but this will not be the case in the future. Instead, the physician will become a "technologist," or technician, who will use new technology to diagnose disease and prevent its spread. Primary care will become prevention and will be turned over to functional/integrative medical doctors. We will embrace chiropractic medicine, massage, acupuncture, and a full complement of preventative medicine. Your current physician will not go away, but the role he or she plays will change, and dramatically so. The health care providers charged with prevention will provide care to the wellderly, while traditional physicians will provide treatment to the illderly.

When making the decision to go to a physician, you need to first determine what type of care you need. If you are already ill and have a specific problem, then you should go to a traditional physician specialist, or illderly provider, e.g., an internist for general internal medicine care, a cardiologist for heart problems, an orthopedist for muscle or joint pain or osteoarthritis, etc. However, if you are looking at preventive measures, then you should consider a functional/integrative physician, naturopath, chiropractor, acupuncturist, or other provider who deals with wellderly care. There is a big difference!

As patients, we need to be proactive in dealing with our health. One problem today is that people are losing faith in their physicians. Statistics back up this growing dismay: Since 1966, according to a Harris Poll, the number of Americans who feel a "great deal" of confidence in their health care providers has dropped nearly 42 percent.

Whether you are seeking wellderly or illderly care, choosing the right physician is a critical step on the road to good health, and it is important to find one with whom you can establish an open and honest dialogue. You should feel comfortable enough to ask your provider any questions without feeling embarrassed. You should also feel confident that your provider has a good working knowledge of your personal medical history and takes the time to both ask you questions and answer yours. You might also want to check the physician's qualifications to see if he or she has an area of specialty. Recommendations from friends also help in determining a physician's expertise and rapport with patients. This may be one of the most critical decisions of your lifetime, and it's good to make it when you are well rather than when you are putting out a medical fire.

Every medical profession is becoming more specialized as a result of the rapid acceleration of new information and education. Medical knowledge is doubling every eight years, and this is expected to drop to every two years in the near future. When it comes to medical professionals, it is critical that they keep up with leading-edge research, new methodologies, and innovative treatments. Your own knowledge about various physicians and their specialties is important, so let's start by talking about the differences between various physicians and how they have been trained.

Allopathic-Traditional Physicians

Allopathic physicians, or MDs, are what we consider to be "traditional" physicians trained in Western medicine. They are an important part of the delivery of health care in America, but they are just one part of that system. As more and more of us look for different answers, the field of alternative/complementary medicine will continue to grow, especially as it relates to wellderly care (allopathic physicians are primarily involved with illderly problems). If you are seeing an allopathic physician, you may want to take the time to write down your questions about specific problems you are having with your health. These doctors may also answer questions on diet, exercise, and lifestyle, depending on whether they take a wider, more holistic view of medical care. Many MDs are more than willing to help you in these areas—you just need to ask.

There are great traditional physicians with a "whole-person" view who are writing books and sponsoring Internet sites that provide excellent information on healthy life choices (Michael F. Roizen, MD; Mehmet C. Oz, MD; Eric R. Braverman, MD; John E. Sarno, MD; and James E. Dowd, MD, to name a few). Look these physicians up on the Internet and buy their books. You will learn a lot about nutrition and natural choices. These practitioners have not turned their backs on traditional medicine: they just realize that good health starts with good diet, good attitude, and exercise. WebMD (www.webmd.com) is another good source of information, and millions of Americans are turning to this site to become informed medical consumers. We are taking our lives back. The best is yet to come as more and more of us decide to live a long and healthy life without prescription drugs.

Functional Medicine and the Future of Health Care

A change in traditional medicine, called functional medicine, is beginning to occur, and this change is good news for all of us. With functional medicine, your physician provides you with personalized medicine that deals with primary prevention and underlying causes instead of the symptoms of serious chronic disease. The following important information is taken from the Web site of the Institute for Functional Medicine (www.functionalmedicine.org).

Functional medicine is anchored by an examination of the core clinical imbalances that underlie various disease conditions. Those imbalances arise as environmental inputs such as diet, nutrients (including air and water), exercise, and trauma are processed by one's body, mind, and spirit through a unique set of genetic predispositions, attitudes, and beliefs. The fundamental physiological processes include communication, both outside and inside the cell; bioenergetics, or the transformation of food into energy; replication, repair, and maintenance of structural integrity, from the cellular to the whole body level; elimination of waste; protection and defense; and transport and circulation.

You can find a physician who practices functional medicine in your area by visiting the Web site above. These physicians are the hope for our future. They should be a destination stop on your journey to good health. I made the change, and I hope you will too. For me the switch has produced important changes in my care. My traditionally trained physician practices integrative (functional) medicine and she has me seeing an oncologist for my ongoing breast cancer testing and exams, an internist for my physical examinations, and a health care specialist who provides my healing touch therapy. She oversees my medical "team" and takes care of my nutrition planning and exercise program. She has provided me with the perfect balance of traditional medical care, coupled with integrative care. Everyone involved in the plan was selected because they support a holistic approach to medicine. I currently take supplements but no prescription drugs.

Osteopathic Physicians

When you visit a physician and you see "DO" instead of "MD" after their name, you may wonder what the difference is, and you are not alone. According to the American Osteopathic Association, a DO is an osteopathic physician and an MD is an allopathic physician. You may not even be aware that these are the only two types of licensed physicians in the United States. Both DOs and MDs are licensed to perform surgery and prescribe medication.

After medical school, both DOs and MDs can choose to practice in a specialty area of medicine such as psychiatry, surgery, or obstetrics. They both complete a residency program, which takes typically two to six years of additional training.

If you are looking for more answers and want to get advice on disease prevention, perhaps an osteopathic physician would be an appropriate choice for you and your family. The "whole person" approach to medical care may just give you the type of second opinion that takes your specific care needs into consideration before drugs are prescribed.

Naturopaths

Traditional medicine has fought to keep medically trained individuals with training in nutrition (called naturopaths) from getting licensed to practice an alternative form of medicine. These doctors have an "ND" after their names and should not be confused with a naturalist. To understand naturopathic medicine you just need to know a little Latin:

**Is there any difference between these two types of physicians?
Yes and no.**

Applicants to both DO and MD colleges typically have a four-year undergraduate degree with an emphasis on science courses.

Both DOs and MDs complete four years of basic medical education.

Both DOs and MDs must pass comparable state licensing examinations.

DOs and MDs both practice in fully accredited and licensed hospitals and medical centers.

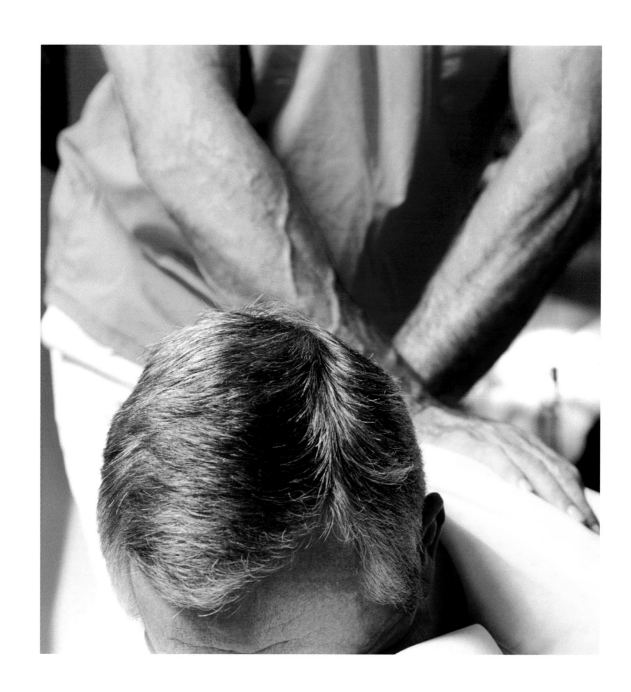

naturopathic medicine focuses on *vis medicatrix naturae*, that is, "the healing power of nature." Naturopaths will most likely start out by helping you improve your diet and lifestyle before suggesting prescription drugs to treat and prevent disease. It is always worth a try to make changes in your diet to improve your health.

Now, for a word of warning: When I say you should seek the opinion of a naturopath, I am defining naturopath as an individual with an academic degree granted by one of the four licensed naturopathic medical schools in the country. I think naturopaths have a lot to offer and I hope that more states will provide them with an avenue to licensure. Fifteen states currently license naturopaths.

Chiropractic

More people now visit chiropractors than traditional physicians. Although chiropractors have not gone through the rigorous schooling that MDs have, they have treated sickness without the use of drugs or surgery for the past 112 years. Chiropractors are known for taking a preventive approach to health care. They do this by focusing on the electrochemical signals that connect your brain to every cell in your body; these signals are regulated through the nervous system and protected by the spine. Chiropractors maintain the proper position of the joints in order to protect the nervous system, and they correct the cause of any interference between the spine and the nerve fibers that may affect your health. Chiropractors also support a totally functioning body by focusing on health wellness, including proper amounts of water, nutrient-rich food, exercise, and emotional well-being.

Acupuncture

A form of medicine that has been practiced in China and other Asian countries for thousands of years, acupuncture has become an increasingly popular form of medical treatment in the U.S. since 1971. There are now estimated to be more than eight million Americans who have used acupuncture. Acupuncture arose out of the Chinese belief in *qi*, a vital life force that is necessary to maintain balance. If your qi is blocked along certain pathways (or meridians), acupuncture—the use of thin metal needles to stimulate certain anatomical points on the body—can unblock the meridians.

Acupuncture aids in preventing disease, which is considered an imbalance in the body, and thus may be considered a valuable form of wellderly care. The FDA regulates the needles used by licensed acupuncture practitioners, and the NIH continue to study the health benefits of acupuncture in such health conditions as chronic low back pain, headaches, and osteoarthritis. There are also continuing efforts to understand the neurological bases for acupuncture treatment, especially as it relates to meridians and needle acupuncture points.

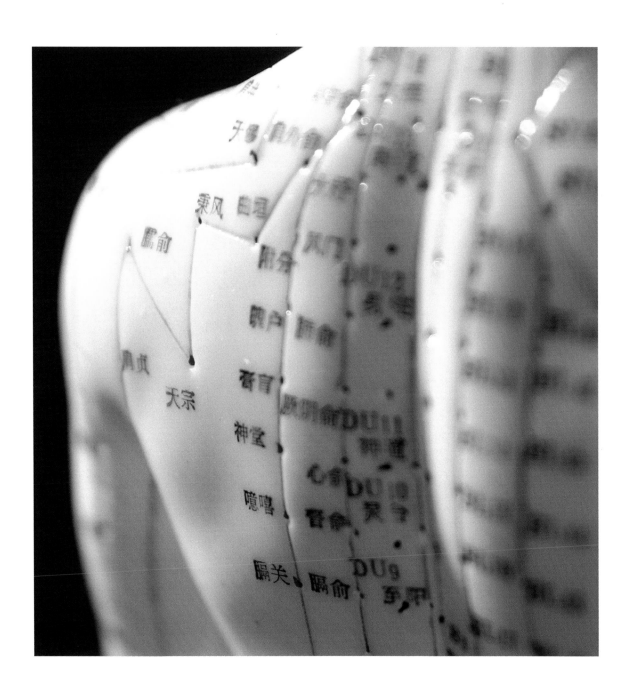

Your Medical Future Is Now

We are now experiencing a fundamental shift in the way health care is dispensed, and it is important for you to be aboard this high-speed train to longevity. Given the fundamental shift in attitude away from pharmaceuticals and toward genetic testing, from mass-prescribed drugs to individualized medicine, and most importantly, from disease care to health care, things look bright. Many choices are available to you now that will help you go forward on this journey.

The most important thing to remember is that, although we are all on the same journey, we may be riding in different cars. As a result, we may not need the same tune-up. It's important to move away from the "one-tune-up-fits-all" notion perpetuated by drug companies and instead fix what's broken in your own body. Technology is going to allow you to reach your goal more efficiently. Although it may be a little scary, just like turning on the computer for the first time was, this is a life-saving journey. All it takes is a shift in attitude and taking small steps along the way. As difficult as the changes are for some of us, it's important to remember that every step is a milestone. Once you realize that you can make small health care and lifestyle choices that really make a difference, you're on the road to Living Well at One Hundred™.

Let's take a look at the ten milestones you can achieve today.

TEN STEPS I AM TAKING ON MY JOURNEY TO GOOD HEALTH

Made a decision to focus on wellness, not disease

Checked my blood test results

Made a list of all my prescription drugs and their dosages

Checked into the possible side effects of various drugs I am taking

Checked to see if my state recognizes licensed naturopathic physicians, and if not, I wrote a letter to my elected representatives about this

Checked WebMD for information about finding a physician

Called my doctor's office and inquired about genetic testing

Wrote down my family history of health issues

Wrote a letter to my elected representative asking him or her to help stop prescription drug advertisements

Read an article about breakthroughs in medical technology

We first make our habits, and then our habits make us.

—John Dryden

CHAPTER FOUR
NUTRITION

Tune Your Engines! Refine Your Fuel!

Chapter 4:NUTRITION

When it comes to taking a journey toward a healthy lifestyle, what you eat is probably one of the most important things to consider. Embarking on our journey involves very simple modifications in your eating habits, and you can start by making just a few changes at a time. Most importantly, these changes lead you on the road to healthy living while at the same time saving you money—and it's still possible for you to eat lavishly and luxuriously like a millionaire!

First, let's look at what you eat. I don't like to use the word "diet" because it implies a short-term plan, while healthy nutrition really involves a lifetime program that gives you choices based on things that you like to eat. There are many food pyramids that provide the basic framework for a balanced diet, the most notable one distributed by the U.S. Department of Agriculture (USDA). Many trust this food pyramid, but I believe that it is better suited to fattening cattle than adding years to our lives. How have we gotten to whatever age we happen to be and still not know what we should and should not be eating? Yes, schools should teach us math, science, and English, but we should also be instructed on how to live a long life by understanding food basics.

Basically, we need to eat less food. We should eat less bread and pasta, add fish to our diets, have fruits and vegetables with every meal, and whenever possible make our food choices organic. Doesn't this sound simple? This is nothing new, but the more we hear the same advice from multiple sources, the more likely we are to have a willing and open mind about what we eat.

Food Pyramids

The USDA developed a food pyramid about forty years ago. Since the "DA" stands for department of agriculture, it makes sense that they did so by working with farmers. This is why the main recommendation for required servings is corn and grain. The pyramid is a great idea for my Iowa farming friends, but not such a good idea when it comes to a healthy diet. With all that is known about the importance of good nutrition, it is amazing that the government still cannot get it right.

Many different food pyramids have been formulated by various organizations, from the Harvard School of Public Health to the World Health Organization. A new food pyramid, called MyPyramid, was released by the USDA in April 2005. The new food pyramid is a tool to educate people about how to eat a more balanced diet from a greater variety of food portions without counting calories. The USDA has now expanded the four food groups to six groups and expanded the number of servings to meet the calorie needs of most people.

A copy of the new food pyramid can be found at mypyramid.gov, where you can tailor your pyramid based on your own personalized program after you insert your height and weight.

The Living Well at One Hundred™ Food Pyramid

I believe that a healthy lifestyle is one in which you don't have to deprive yourself, so I have devised a significantly different and effective food pyramid, one that, believe it or not, includes chocolate, red wine, and other "no-nos" from other so-called diet plans—after all, I promised that we were going to have fun on our journey to good health and longevity! Eating the things we enjoy is one of the pleasures in life that none of us should have to forego. There have been many changes in the way we look at food that used to be considered "bad" for us. We needn't worry anymore about sacrificing or giving up many of our favorite foods. Using new research to back up my food pyramid, I have discovered the many health benefits of our favorite treats. For example, among commonly consumed foods, chocolate has the highest concentration of flavonoids, a rich source of antioxidants. Dark chocolate is cheaper than therapy, and you don't need an appointment. As for wine, Harvard researchers have listed moderate alcohol consumption as one of the "eight proven ways to reduce coronary heart disease risk."

"There was a time when I had to actually EAT the chocolate before it went straight to my hips!"

Wine makes daily living easier, less hurried,
with fewer tensions and more tolerance.

—Benjamin Franklin

Living Well at One Hundred™ Food Pyramid ©McCord Research 2009

FROM FORBIDDEN TO FANTASTIC

A Chocoholic's Dream Come True

Most of us have never had a piece of chocolate we didn't like, but for years chocolate was considered a taboo item on everyone's food list. But not anymore: according to the latest research, flavanols, an antioxidant compound found in cocoa, help to reduce free radicals, clear artery walls, and increase blood flow to the brain. At Johns Hopkins University School of Medicine, researchers found that eating a few squares of chocolate per day can decrease your risk of having a heart attack by nearly one-half. At the Salk Institute for Biological Studies, studies done with mice found that the specific flavanol found in chocolate (epicatechin) improved memory and brain function in the hippocampus. Dark chocolate was also shown to improve insulin sensitivity in healthy persons, according to an Italian Health Department study. Cocoa may thus aid in battling cardiovascular disease, diabetes, and brain disorders such as dementia. Besides, having a little piece of chocolate will help satisfy that craving that oftentimes hits during the day. It stimulates the production of endorphins, which gives a feeling of pleasure, and produces serotonin, which acts as an antidepressant.

But before you devour a giant Hershey's bar or a scoop of double fudge ice cream, it's important to note that the recommended serving size for chocolate is 1½ ounces, or slightly smaller than the size of your two thumbs. There's also a hierarchy of chocolate that is considered good for you, depending on the amount of cocoa it contains—just because it's chocolate doesn't necessarily mean it's good for you. Checking the ingredient list is important. Generally, the more cocoa, the more flavanols, so look for chocolate that contains a minimum of 35 percent cocoa. Also, check the ingredient list to make sure there is no vegetable oil or hydrogenated oil, but rather cocoa butter. As for chocolate drink mixes, if the cocoa is treated with alkali, it usually destroys the flavanol compounds in cocoa, so be sure to check that on the label as well.

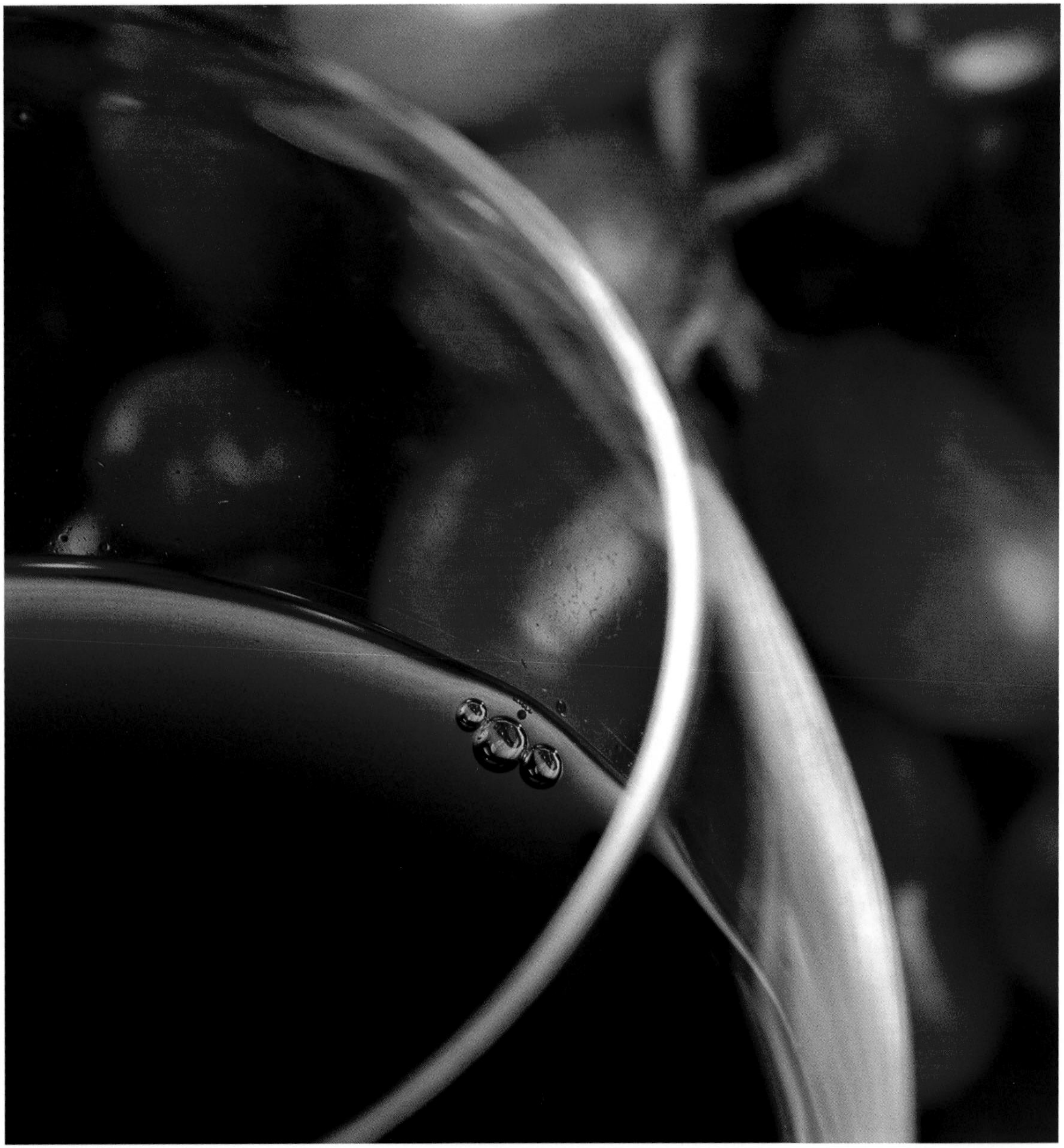

Nothing to Wine About

Do you want to relax after a long day at work? Now you can pour that glass of red wine, sit back, and enjoy more than just its relaxation benefits. Current research has shown that moderate alcohol consumption is a proven way of reducing coronary heart disease risk, with red wine being the most beneficial to heart health. Not only is wine good for your heart, but also like chocolate (which is rich in flavonoids), it can aid in the treatment of neurological diseases such as Alzheimer's disease and Parkinson's disease. Flavonoids not only reduce the production of LDL and stimulate the production of HDL, but they also lead to reduced blood clotting.

A pivotal study published several years ago in the journal *Nature* found that red wine inhibited the synthesis of a protein called endothelin-1 that can lead to the development of atherosclerosis, a buildup of fatty material along artery walls. Further studies also linked red wine with high levels of procyanidin, a type of polyphenol, or antioxidant, found in the skin of grapes; this antioxidant helps to protect blood vessels.

Researchers at Harvard Medical School and the NIH have reported that the antioxidant resveratrol, a type of polyphenol again found in the skin and seeds of red grapes, was shown to inhibit tumor development in some cancers. At Mount Sinai School of Medicine in New York, research showed that moderate wine consumption in mice helped prevent plaque buildup in the brain; this buildup is a characteristic of Alzheimer's disease.

The dryer the wine, the more flavonoid benefits, so Cabernet Sauvignon, Petit Syrah and Pinot Noir wines are at the top of the list; white wine has significantly smaller amounts of flavonoids than its red counterpart. Again, serving size is important: the recommended amount to reap the most benefit is 4 ounces for women and 4-8 ounces for men.

Go Nuts for Nuts

Many of us have been led to believe that eating nuts is going to make us fat—at one time they were considered too oily, rich, and high in calories. In fact, as the FDA found in 2003, a handful of nuts a day has been shown to reduce the risk of heart disease. That's because most of the fat in nuts is monounsaturated and polyunsaturated, which has been shown to lower levels of LDL (so-called bad cholesterol). Other diseases, such as type 2 (non-insulin-dependent) diabetes, dementia, macular degeneration, and gallstones have also been shown to be positively affected by the regular consumption of nuts. In fact, if you eat nuts regularly, you can expect to add two years to your life span.

Not all nuts are as beneficial as others: walnuts, almonds, peanuts, pistachios, pecans, and hazelnuts are on the list of "good" nuts, while cashews, Brazil nuts, and macadamia nuts contain relatively high levels of saturated fats and so should be eaten sparingly. Walnuts are particularly good for us because they have high levels of omega-3 fatty acids that other nuts don't have. One study showed that people who ate a handful of almonds every day reduced their LDL cholesterol by 4.4 percent. In July 2003 the FDA approved the first qualified

health claim for a food for use on package labels, which states, "Scientific evidence suggests but does not prove that eating 1.5 ounces per day of most nuts, such as almonds, as part of a diet low in saturated fat and cholesterol, may reduce the risk of heart disease."

It's best to eat raw nuts rather than those that are coated in oils and salt. If you consume your 1.5 ounces a day, you're likely to reduce your chances not only of cardiovascular disease, but Alzheimer's and cancer as well; this is because of the high levels of vitamin E, a powerful antioxidant, as well as magnesium, calcium, and iron all found in nuts.

There is good news, too, for those of us who used to think nuts were fattening. It has been shown, somewhat surprisingly, that people who eat nuts are more likely to keep their weight down, according to a Loma Linda University study of thirty-one thousand people. As cited in the *American Journal of Clinical Nutrition*, there have been instances of increased metabolic rates associated with the consumption of nuts. It also noted that nuts appear to satisfy hunger, and that fact may very well lead to reduced consumption of other less-healthy foods.

Get Your Fruits and Vegetables

You can also use the following guidelines to help you choose fruits and vegetables with plenty of nutrients. Remember, it's all about making your own choices. You don't have to eat broccoli if you don't want to, but you can choose sweet red peppers or a vegetable juice cocktail instead. If you don't like spinach, eat almonds as your source of vitamin E. Oatmeal is a good nondairy source of calcium if you don't particularly like dairy products. Here are some general guidelines for getting the best sources of nutrients from fruits and vegetables.

Nutrients Found in Fruits and Vegetables

Sources of Vitamin A
Bright orange vegetables such as carrots, sweet potatoes, and pumpkin
Tomatoes and tomato products, and red sweet peppers
Leafy greens such as spinach, collards, turnip greens, kale, beet and mustard greens, green leaf and romaine lettuces
Orange fruits such as mangoes, cantaloupes, apricots, and red or pink grapefruits

Sources of Vitamin C
Citrus fruits and juices, kiwi fruit, strawberries, guavas, papayas, and cantaloupes
Broccoli, peppers, tomatoes, cabbage (especially Chinese cabbage), brussels sprouts, and potatoes
Leafy greens such as romaine, turnip greens, and spinach

Sources of Folate
Cooked dry beans and peas
Oranges and orange juice
Deep green leaves such as spinach and mustard greens

Sources of Potassium
Baked white or sweet potatoes
Cooked greens (such as spinach), and winter (orange) squash
Bananas, plantains, many dried fruits, oranges and orange juice, cantaloupes, and honeydew melons
Cooked dry beans, soybeans, tomato products (sauce, paste, and puree), beet greens

Fabulous Fibers

What do fresh fruits, vegetables, whole grains, seeds, and nuts have in common? All are plant foods that are considered dietary sources of fiber. Dietary fiber is involved in the breakdown of starch in the large intestine, which aids in digestion. Soluble fiber—found in beans, fruits, oat bran, and vegetables—helps you feel full by slowing the passage of food through the intestines. Insoluble fiber—found in wheat bran, whole grains, vegetables, and beans—keeps your digestive system regular.

Colon cancer is but one disease associated with inadequate fiber intake. Researchers at Harvard Medical School found that men who consumed only 12 grams of fiber a day were twice as likely to develop precancerous colon changes as men whose daily fiber intake was about 30 grams. Scientists theorize that insoluble fiber adds bulk to stools and may in turn affect the transit of carcinogens through the lower intestines and out of the body. As for breast cancer, data from the Nurse's Health Study noted no significant link between fiber intake and cancer risk in middle-aged women; however, in the early stages, fiber may reduce the growth of breast tumors circulating in the bloodstream by binding with estrogen and preventing excess estrogen from being reabsorbed.

Digestive disorders such as constipation have been shown to be positively affected by fiber intake as the fiber hastens the passage of fecal material through the gut. Fiber also may help reduce the risk of diverticulosis, a condition in which small pouches form in the colon wall. People who already have diverticulosis often find that increased fiber consumption can alleviate symptoms, which include constipation and/or diarrhea, abdominal pain, flatulence, and mucus or blood in stool.

Soluble fiber traps carbohydrates to slow their digestion and absorption; in theory, this may help prevent wide swings in blood sugar levels throughout the day. Additionally, a new study from the Harvard School of Public Health suggests that a high-sugar, low-fiber diet more than doubles women's risk of type 2 diabetes. In the Harvard study, cereal fiber was associated with a 28 percent decreased risk of diabetes, while fiber from fruits and vegetables had no effect. In comparison, cola beverages, white bread, white rice, and French fries increased the risk.

Clinical studies show that a heart-healthy diet (low in saturated fat and cholesterol and high in fruits, vegetables, and grain products that contain soluble fiber) can lower blood cholesterol. Because soluble fiber binds to dietary cholesterol, it helps to reduce blood cholesterol levels; this in turn reduces cholesterol deposits in the artery walls. There also is evidence that soluble fiber can slow the manufacture of cholesterol in the liver.

Recent findings from two long-term, large-scale studies of men suggest that high fiber intake can significantly lower the risk of heart attack. Men who ate the most fiber-rich foods (35 grams a day, on average) suffered one-third fewer heart attacks than those who had the lowest fiber intake (15 grams a day), according to a Finnish study of 21,903 male smokers aged fifty to sixty-nine. Findings from an ongoing U.S. study of 43,757 male health professionals (some of whom were sedentary, overweight, or smokers) suggest that those who ate more than 25 grams of fiber per day had a

36 percent lower risk of developing heart disease than those who consumed less than 15 grams daily. This study noted that for each 10 grams of fiber added to the diet; the risk of heart failure was decreased by 29 percent.

If you want to lose weight, bear in mind that insoluble fiber has been shown to provide few calories because it passes quickly through the body. Insoluble fiber also may hamper the absorption of calorie-dense dietary fat. Fiber-rich foods are more filling than other foods, so people tend to eat less of them.

The American Dietetic Association now recommends a minimum of 20 to 35 grams of fiber a day for a healthy adult, or 14 grams per 1,000 calories. It is estimated that, on average, we only consume about half that amount.

Get on the Grain Train

Because of the proven health benefits of a diet rich in fiber, the USDA has provided guidelines for fiber-rich products. On your journey to health, you might want to hop on the train provided by the USDA guidelines. When it comes to grain products, it is important to note that the amount of fiber in your diet may be affected by processing. There are two types of grain products: whole and refined. Whole grains include the entire grain kernel: the outer shell, or bran, is a source of B vitamins and trace minerals, while the germ provides nourishment for the seed and contains antioxidants, vitamin E, and B vitamins.

Have You Tried Whole-Grain Versions of these Foods?

- » Bagels
- » Barley
- » Bread
- » Breakfast cereal
- » Bulgur
- » Cakes and cookies
- » Cornbread
- » Couscous
- » Crackers
- » English muffins
- » Graham crackers
- » Grits
- » Muffins
- » Noodles
- » Oatmeal
- » Pancakes and waffles
- » Pita bread
- » Popcorn
- » Pretzels
- » Rice
- » Rolls and buns
- » Pasta
- » Tortillas

You can identify whole grain products by reading the ingredient list on the food label: the whole grain should be the first ingredient listed. Foods that carry the "whole grain" label must contain 51 percent or more whole grains by weight and be low in fat. Don't be fooled by food products that are said to be "multigrain," "stone-ground," "100 percent wheat," "cracked wheat," "seven-grain," or "bran." The following are all whole grains:

- » Brown rice
- » Bulgur
- » Graham flour
- » Oatmeal
- » Pearl barley
- » Popcorn
- » Whole-grain corn
- » Whole oats
- » Whole rye
- » Whole wheat
- » Wild rice

Try to Avoid these Products Made with Refined Grain

- » Enriched bread
- » Wheat flour
- » White rice

Chapter 4 | Nutrition | 92

Ten Tips to Add More Fiber to Your Diet

»   Cook with whole grains by adding beans to soup, vegetables to spaghetti sauce, whole grain bread or crackers to meatloaf, or brown rice to stuffing.

»   Bake oatmeal raisin cookies.

»   Try a fruit smoothie with fresh or frozen fruit, low-fat yogurt, and fruit juice.

»

»   Eat vegetables raw to preserve fiber content, or cook them in a microwave, which retains more nutrients than cooking them slowly.

»   Sprinkle whole grain cereal on your favorite dessert.

»   Stock your shelves with whole-grain products such as brown rice and whole-grain pasta.

»   Get more fiber with a delicious fruit salad sprinkled with walnuts and shredded, unsweetened coconut.

»   Switch to corn tortillas, which have 50 percent more fiber than flour tortillas.

»   Use vegetables to top your favorite meat or fish.

»   Take a fiber supplement that can be added to drinks and your favorite recipes with no added flavor or texture. Usually 11 grams of a fiber supplement contains just four calories. I put my fiber product into my morning coffee; no taste, no texture, no problem.

You can use the following chart to list your favorite fruits and vegetables and take it with you when you go grocery shopping.

FRUITS AND VEGETABLES I LIKE

Fruits I like (write down the fruits you like).

_____

_____

_____

_____

_____

Vegetables I like (write down the vegetables you like).

_____

_____

_____

_____

Write down when you could eat each of these fruits and vegetables throughout the day. Try to make sure you choose a variety.

_____

_____

_____

_____

_____

_____

_____

BREAKFAST:

_____

_____

_____

LUNCH:

_____

_____

_____

DINNER:

_____

_____

_____

SNACK:

_____

_____

DESSERT:

_____

_____

Good Fat and Bad Fat

It may be hard to believe for those of us who hate the word "fat," but fat is a chemical compound that is essential to your body. The body does not manufacture the three essential fatty acids, so you must get them from food sources. Fat is also necessary for the absorption of certain vitamins. The biggest problem we face is not whether or not we eat fat: it's what kind of fat we eat and how much.

Although all fats have the same number of calories, they differ in how they affect you. Saturated fats and trans fats should be avoided as they can produce aging of the arteries. Saturated fat is fat found in animal products such as red meat and dairy products, including butter and cheese. There are also plant sources of saturated fat, mainly coconut oil, palm kernel oil, palm oil, and cocoa butter.

Polyunsaturated and monounsaturated fats are primarily found in nuts, seeds, fish, and oils from plants; these fats may help in lowering blood cholesterol. "Good," or polyunsaturated fat can actually have a positive effect on the disease that the bad fat is said to cause. These polyunsaturated fats are often a good source of omega-3 fatty acids, found mostly in cold-water fish, nuts, oils, seeds, and also in dark leafy greens, flaxseed oils, and some vegetable oils. Omega-3 fatty acids are also known as essential fatty acids because our bodies need them, but our bodies do not manufacture them; so our diet and supplements are the

only sources. Omega-3 fatty acids are thought to lower blood pressure, combat LDL cholesterol, fight inflammation, and protect the brain and nervous system. Olive oil and canola oil are the best examples of healthy oils. It is important to remember that all fat contains 120 calories per tablespoon, so try to limit your intake of fat to approximately 25 percent of your total calorie consumption. Regardless of whether it is a "good" fat or a "bad" fat, you should be sure not to overdo your intake of it.

Just as it is important to have enough motor oil in your car, our nutritional plan demands that you maintain proper levels of the right kinds of oil in your body. On our journey, you need to strive for the most efficient and least dangerous levels of oil to enjoy the ride.

Simple Switches

Easy substitutions that will have little affect on taste can make a big difference in your health quotient. If changing what you eat seems overwhelming and difficult, remember that you can just make a few upgrades that will charge your engine and allow you to travel on the road to good health with very little effort.

Replace		Replacement
White potatoes	with	Sweet potatoes
Croutons	with	Walnuts
Mayonnaise	with	Avocado
Button mushrooms	with	Shiitake mushrooms
Milk chocolate	with	Dark chocolate
Iceberg lettuce	with	Romaine lettuce
Cream cheese	with	Almond butter
All-purpose flour	with	Whole-wheat flour
Vegetable oil	with	Olive oil
Sour cream	with	Yogurt

There are many more diet substitutions that allow you to focus on good things to add to your diet without making you feel like you're sacrificing a thing: for example, substitute tuna packed in oil with white tuna packed in water. Simply changing from a creamy salad dressing to a delicious oil-and-vinegar topping can save calories without sacrificing taste, or use mustard or salsa to flavor your burger instead of mayonnaise and ketchup.

Just look inside the following refrigerators to see how simple switches of the following items can make a nutritional difference and also cut fat and calories from your daily food plan.

GOOD REFRIGERATOR	BAD REFRIGERATOR
Omega-3 eggs	Standard eggs
Dark beer	Light beer
Olive oil dressing	Creamy dressing
Mustard, low-sodium soy sauce, salsa	Ketchup and mayonnaise
Organic fat-free milk	2 percent milk
Pomegranate or cranberry juice and club soda	Sugary fruit drinks
Natural peanut butter and fruit spread	Standard peanut butter and jelly
Part-skim mozzarella	Brie or cheddar
Transfat-free spread	Butter
Sweet potatoes or red-skinned potatoes	White potatoes
Whole-grain pasta	Refined pasta
Berries, kiwi, melon	Green grapes
Romaine lettuce	Iceberg lettuce
Whole-grain bread	White bread

Splurge on a Dinner Out

Eating out is a way to spoil yourself and relax after a hectic day. Many restaurants are responding to the health needs of their patrons, with some even listing low-fat, low-sodium, or low-calorie items or "heart-friendly" dishes. If the restaurant doesn't have what you want or you are concerned about food preparation just let your server know what you want. Some ideas:

» If you don't know the serving size of your selection, ask the server.
» Try to eat the same (small) portion as you would at home; share with your dinner partner or ask to take the rest home.
» Eat slowly.
» Ask for fish or meat broiled with no extra butter.
» Order a baked potato plain with sour cream to the side, instead of adding butter.
» If you are on a low-sodium diet, ask that no salt be added to your food.
» Order all salad dressings, sauces, and gravies on the side, and use them sparingly.
» Ask for substitutions, such as salad instead of French fries.
» Stay away from breaded or fried foods.

Believe it or not, you can even eat out at a fast food restaurant as long as you keep the following guidelines in mind:

» If you're having a fast food meal, be sure that your other meals that day contain healthier foods, such as fruits and vegetables.
» Think about how the food is cooked. Broiled, not fried!
» Know the nutritional value of the foods you order; most fast food items are high in fat and calories. Most fast food restaurants now have the information posted.
» Know that an average fast food meal can run as high as 2,000 calories or more.
» Watch out for words such as "jumbo," "giant," "deluxe," or "super-sized."
» Stay away from double burgers or super hot dogs with extra cheese.

» If there is a salad bar, avoid things such as bacon bits, cheese, and croutons.

» Pizza can be a good choice as long as it has thin crust with vegetable toppings; avoid pizza with extra cheese and meats.

Most of us like to snack, and oftentimes snacks are an important part of staying well fueled. But when it comes to snacks, you can also cut calories without depriving yourself. Again, simple switches are all you need to keep from consuming those extra 150 calories a day.

Switch from

Hershey's bar	to	M&Ms
Peanut butter	to	Cream cheese
Seedless grapes	to	Grape tomatoes
Tortilla chips	to	Pretzels

Another tip: When snacking, measure out the correct amount for a single serving, put it on a plate or in a bowl, and put away that large bag. If you do have a treat, eat it slowly and enjoy it.

Going Organic

A journey toward good health and longevity is in many ways about choosing a new destination—it involves getting off the road to "chemicals" and on the road to "nutrients" and "organic." Organic food has been defined by the USDA as food produced by farmers who emphasize the use of renewable resources and the conservation of soil and water. Organic meat, poultry, eggs, and dairy products come from animals that are given no antibiotics or growth hormones. Organic food is produced without using most conventional pesticides; fertilizers made with synthetic ingredients or sewage sludge; bioengineering; or ionizing radiation. Before a product can be labeled "organic," a government-approved certifier inspects the farm where the food is grown to make sure the farmer is complying with USDA organic standards. Companies that handle or process organic food before it gets to your local supermarket or restaurant must also be certified.

The good news is that most of us (including the First Family's organic garden) have already started to change our course. Who would have imagined just a decade ago that the organic foods industry would have grown to the size it is today? No longer are we limited to a few products that are hard to find: today organic is mainstream, and a bounty of healthy foods and products can be found in grocery stores across America. Organic food is good for us and it is also good for the earth. As stewards of this planet we need to stop putting toxins in our soil and waterways. Join those that have found a healthier life by buying their food from local farmers, cooperatives, and community gardens.

Let's look at the trend toward eating organic. In the decade between 1997 and 2007, sales of organic food grew by nearly 80 percent, to $17.7 billion. This change in direction was fueled by millions of shoppers looking for healthier and safer foods that are environmentally friendly. Today nearly 60 percent of U.S. households buy some organic items. The demand for organic products is expected to grow as people place more of a premium on eating nutritious food and maintaining a healthy lifestyle. While some organic foods may cost 10 to 20 percent more than their non-organic competitors (stay tuned: prices are coming down), we now understand that the health savings gained from organic foods are tremendous and in fact may be lifesaving. Safeway grocery stores launched its own organic line of food under the O label.

Currently at 150 products, the brand is expected to be expanded by Safeway to 300 products by early 2009. SuperValu's acquisition of the Albertson's grocery store chain in 2006 made SuperValu the second-largest grocery store chain in America. While Albertson's previously carried about fifty organic products under the Nature's Best brand, under the SuperValu flagship that number was expected to expand to more than three hundred products.

It isn't just the grocery store chains that have gotten the message. Costco is a great destination if you are looking for organic food—they have everything from organic coffee to organic produce. Sam's Club and WalMart are also developing a good selection of organic products, including those sold under their private-label selections. This indicates that grocery store chains and discount warehouse chains are moving quickly to capture the growing consumer interest in organic foods. Organic food accounted for just $3.6 billion of the U.S. market in 1997, but by 2004 it generated $11.9 billion; that number rose to $13.8 billion in 2005. In 2007, sales of organic products reached $17.7 billion, so you can see that we are headed in the right direction.

This change is not driven by industry or the grocery stores: people like you are driving it. Slowly, the more we read and learn, the more we realize that the pesticides, antibiotics, and hormones that have been pumped into our food are not healthy—in fact, they are dangerous. Millions of Americans (and people around the world) have incorporated at least some organic items into their food and product selections.

Most people think that buying organic products costs more, but since large supermarket chains began adding their own organic product lines, that notion is changing. Compare, for example, the prices of non-organic versus organic products that we found at a Ralph's grocery store in Los Angeles in late 2008:

	NON-ORGANIC	ORGANIC
Milk, ½ gal.	$3.69	$3.49
Grape juice, 46 oz.	$3.29	$3.59
Butter, 1 lb.	$5.49	$5.99
Peanut butter, 16 oz.	$3.49	$3.49
Canned tomatoes	$2.19	$2.29
Raspberries, 8 oz.	$3.99	$5.99
Romaine lettuce	$3.49	$3.99
Red bell pepper	$2.58	$2.73
0.43 lb @ 5.99/lb.		
Tomatoes	$1.29	$1.20
0.43 @2.99/lb.		
Carrots	$1.99	$1.79
Lemon	$1.49	$1.49
0.49 @1.99/lb.		
Navel orange	$0.98	$0.80
Cilantro	$0.89	$1.39
Dried penne pasta, 16 oz.	$3.49	$1.19
	_____	
	$38.34	**$39.82**

Items purchased on 8/23/2008 at Ralph's Fresh Fare

For only $1.48 more—less than 5 percent of the total bill— we were able to buy all organic products found on an average list of grocery items. You only have to spend very little more to buy organic products.

A good place to find the tastiest, least expensive, and healthiest organic produce is at your local farmer's markets. Most fruits and vegetables in supermarkets are picked before they are ripe, and as a consequence they do not have time to acquire all their vitamins and minerals. Food that has been picked locally contains more important fresh nutrients—up to 59 percent more than food shipped miles and miles to travel from farm to grocery store to your table. You can also talk directly to the farmers to find out what's in season and even get ideas on how to cook the lovely food you're buying.

If you are reluctant to buy all organic products or shop at your local farmer's markets, consider this: fruits and vegetables contain varying amounts of toxic chemicals, chemicals that have been shown to cause everything from dizziness to cancer; much depends on how the fruit is treated and how much of the toxic compounds (usually pesticides) it has absorbed. The following chart shows the nine least toxic and nine most toxic fruits and vegetables.

Nine Fruits and Vegetables With the Least Amounts of Pesticide Residue

Nine Fruits and Vegetables With the Most Amounts of Pesticide Residue

Peaches

Apples

Peppers

Strawberries

Cherries

Lettuce

Grapes

Pears

Potatoes

Just as cars running on the right kind of fuel get better gas mileage, we can live longer and better lives by putting the right kind of fuel in our bodies. There is no one thing that you must do today to change your fuel plan. We want you to make small, easy changes, and if you don't want to change anything at all today, that's fine, too—just start by reading our suggestions and learning a little about what nutritional choices are there for you. Remember, every change you make is a milestone.

If you don't know where you are going,
you will probably end up somewhere else.

—Laurence Johnson Peter

TEN STEPS I AM TAKING ON MY JOURNEY TO GOOD HEALTH

Bought bananas at the grocery store instead of strawberries

Sprinkled an ounce of almonds on my morning cereal

Bought romaine lettuce instead of iceberg

Poured my orange juice into a crystal champagne glass for breakfast

Looked up where to find my local farmer's market

Ate spaghetti with whole-wheat pasta

Used olive oil to make salad dressing

Bought organic peaches

Sat down and had a 4-ounce glass of wine when I came home from work

Finished my day with a piece of dark chocolate

Never eat anything you can't lift.

—Miss Piggy

FOOD PORTIONS

Size Matters

Chapter 5: FOOD PORTIONS

While living well is not about depriving yourself of foods you like, it is also not about eating too much. It is important to control how much you eat as well as choose what you eat; in this way, you will be better able to control the proper amount of nutrients in your daily diet. There are two common situations with portion control: we either think it is impossible to get the recommended four servings of fruits and vegetables in our daily diets, or we are eating way too much food. Most of us are used to living in a "supersized" society, where huge plates of pasta, double servings of French fries, or giant slabs of ribs are the norm for restaurants and fast food franchises. We have lost our ability to gauge what a portion size looks like.

Before we start, it is important to note that the USDA notes proper serving sizes on food labels for the purpose of giving people appropriate nutritional information. All food labels contain serving size information so that products can be standardized, but proper serving sizes are also recommended as nutritional guidelines in dietary plans. These recommendations are suggested not only for weight control, but also to give you information on maintaining the proper nutrient levels for good health.

For those of you who cannot imagine eating the recommended four servings of fruits a day, consider the following: Do you know what 4 ounces of juice, which is considered a single serving of fruit, really looks like? Compare a serving of orange juice with 8 ounces in your typical cup. You think that all of these servings equal a lot of juice, but it's so little that you're going to think your glass is empty.

Remember, you can also get a daily serving of fruit from a blended juice. If you drink it from an 8-ounce glass, you can get nearly all four recommended servings of fruit in one glass. Or better yet, take ½ cup of fruit juice and see how it fills only a tiny fraction of your standard drinking glass. One full glass of fruit juice, or the 8-ounce size commonly served in most restaurants, nearly meets your daily requirement for fruit. Other tips for getting your daily serving of fruit is to put your fruit in a blender, then freeze the puree in your ice cube tray and use the ice to make iced tea. If you've used several fruits for the ice cubes, you're done for the day!

To test your knowledge about what one serving of vegetables should look like, cut up some carrots and place them in a ½-cup measuring cup. Look at how this amount of vegetables looks on a large dinner plate.

If we don't know how small one serving of carrots looks, we also probably have no idea how little it takes to get our daily intake of vegetables. For example, consider a standard-sized cooking pot. Here we have a 3-ounce pot that could hold three whole servings of vegetables—again, nearly the total amount you need for the day.

Getting your daily requirement of fruits and vegetables is actually the easiest part of your food plan.

No More Supersize

Unfortunately, we live in a supersized society. A marketing term developed by David Wallerstein at McDonald's in the 1990s, "supersizing" originally meant adding dramatically to the size of a meal; in this way, customers could order one large portion instead of several smaller portions. The concept behind supersizing was that people did not want to appear gluttonous by ordering several servings so they would rather order one larger, single portion. The result: instead of getting enough fruits and vegetables, we are consuming more of everything else, much of which may not be good for us. Portion sizes have continued to dramatically increase in restaurants and fast food establishments over the years to the point that we now have a supersized notion of what constitutes a serving. To get a sense of what a daily serving really looks like, start by getting out your measuring cups. Put some cooked rice into a ½ cup measure, and then transfer it to your everyday cups and dishes. Now take a look at what that portion looks like. I think you will be surprised at how small the portion is.

Now look at the serving sizes recommended in the following chart, which lists the portions needed for a 2,000-calorie-a-day dietary plan.

Food Groups	2,000-Calorie-Eating Plan	Serving Size
Grains	6–8 servings	1 slice bread
		1 ounce dry cereal
		½ cup cooked rice, pasta, or cereal
Vegetables	4–5 servings	1 cup raw leafy vegetables
		½ cup raw or cooked vegetables
		½ cup vegetable juice
Fruits	4–5 servings	½ cup fruit juice
		1 medium fruit
		¼ cup dried fruit
		½ cup fresh, frozen, or canned fruit
Fat-free or low-fat milk and equivalent milk products	2–3 servings	1 ½ ounce fat-free, low-fat, or reduced-fat cheese
		1 cup fat-free or low-fat yogurt
		1 cup fat-free or low-fat milk
Lean meats, poultry, and fish	2 or fewer servings	3 ounce cooked meat, poultry, or fish
Nuts, seeds, and legumes	4–5 servings per week	1/3 cup or 1½ ounces nuts
		2 tablespoons peanut butter
		2 tablespoons or ½ ounces seeds
		½ cup cooked dry beans or peas

You can use visual guidelines to determine what a serving size looks like. For example, ½ cup of pasta should be the same size as a tennis ball cut in half, as should one medium-sized piece of fruit (not the extra-large-sized ones in your grocery store). Three ounces of meat or fish is visually the same size as a deck of cards. One cup of yogurt or milk equals the size of your fist. For a serving size of oatmeal, you can visualize an ice cream scoop. Two tablespoons of peanut butter equal the size of a ping-pong ball.

Because most of us are so used to eating the large portions being served in restaurants today, the biggest challenge in controlling your weight is determining exactly how much you should be eating. A shocking statistic: gaining ten pounds a year is as simple as eating 150 extra calories per day. For those of us who are watching what we eat, 150 calories looks like the following:

150 Calories   =   1 ounce of potato chips

12 ounces of Coca Cola

25 peanuts

½ cup fast food hashed browns

6 pieces of Bit-O'-Honeys

2 pieces of Demet's Turtles

2 tablespoons blue cheese dressing

Reference: thecaloriecounter.com

Restaurants typically serve double or triple portions, and food manufacturers also sell packages of food products in containers that far exceed our needs. Muffins, for example, which most consider a better food choice than donuts, used to be only 2 inches in diameter—now they are double that size, tripling the number of calories in one muffin.

Labeling is also very deceptive: we think that the calorie content as listed is the total calorie content for that individual-sized bottle or package, when in fact the calorie count is for one serving size. You could be consuming two, three, or even four servings in one package!

Since few of us carry around a measuring cup or spoon when we're about to eat something, consider using your own hands and fingers to determine proper portion sizes. Some examples:

One closed fist	=	1 cup of beverage, cereal, or vegetables
One hand cupped	=	½ cup of pasta, rice, fruit, or beans
Palm of the hand	=	3 ounces of cooked meat or fish
Two thumbs together	=	1 tablespoon of butter, salad dressing, or mayonnaise
One thumb	=	1 ounce of cheese

Switch Plates

Have you ever noticed that American plates are much larger than European plates? Eating on larger plates means eating more food because we almost always eat everything that's on our plates; bigger plates also make our portions look smaller. By simply switching from a dinner plate to a salad plate, you can actually consume 25 percent less. At the same time, it looks as if you are eating more. The same goes for glasses, bowls, and even pots and pans. If you'd rather use a full-sized plate, think about this: You can have a nice salad with mixed greens, ½ cup of tomatoes, ½ ounce of almonds or pecans, and put it on the same plate as one serving of vegetables and a 3-ounce piece of chicken. If you don't use a separate salad plate, you can serve a beautiful, healthy meal on a large plate without eating any extra calories.

Eat Like a Millionaire

A new eating plan does not mean that you have to deprive yourself. On the contrary, you can eat well just by cutting your portion sizes and presenting your meals as if you were dining luxuriously at the best restaurant in town. You deserve to experience this life of luxury. By making better choices, you can spend less money and still eat the finest of meals in an enjoyable way.

Eating well is about making the choice to buy smaller amounts. You can spend the same amount of money and get a perfect 3-ounce filet mignon rather than an 8-ounce round steak; you can have an organic roasted chicken from the finest market for the same price as a bucket of chicken from Kentucky Fried Chicken. Cutting quantities does not mean cutting taste—in fact, by doing so you can allow yourself the opportunity to eat higher-quality food. For example, you don't have to eat a giant Snickers bar to satisfy your craving for chocolate when you can get the same pleasure (and fewer calories) from a piece of Godiva chocolate.

Picture what one serving of meat or fish (3 ounces), two servings of vegetables (½ cup of carrots and ½ cup of peas), and one slice of bread look like served on a 9-inch dinner plate. If it looks sparse, then take out your prettiest china salad plate and enjoy your meal on it instead. Add 3 ounces of wine served in a fine crystal goblet and you've discovered a way to eat less and enjoy food more.

You deserve the very best. There are so many ways to eat well and live rich just by thinking rich. You deserve that fine cut of meat, a beautiful bowl of sweet cherries, a small but fine piece of European chocolate, a small serving of gourmet French cheese, or a taste of olive tapenade. Remember: You don't have to buy a container of small strawberries—instead, find one or two big beautiful strawberries, dip them in a small amount of dark chocolate, and serve them on a crystal plate. Use another beautiful plate to set out two large pieces of shrimp with a healthy dollop of cocktail sauce. Serve whole-wheat toast or crackers with a small amount of gourmet preserves (especially those with reduced sugar), or top them with an olive layered with fine cheese. Accompany this lovely repast with a champagne glass of brewed iced tea, which is filled with healthy antioxidants.

Eat at the Finest Restaurants

To maintain a healthy diet you don't have to deny yourself the pleasure of eating in fine restaurants. We want you to enjoy a luxurious and satisfying life, and we believe you can have a fine dining experience without spending more money than it costs to eat at the Cheesecake Factory or Olive Garden. You can always order a salad and appetizer at an expensive restaurant for the same price as an entrée at a less expensive one—not only do you get a beautiful meal, but you are eating the correct portion size as well. Why pay $25 at a chain restaurant for a dinner that includes a giant steak, a large scoop of mashed potatoes, and a huge salad doused in dressing when for the same amount of money you can have a beautiful petit filet mignon at a five-star restaurant? You can treat yourself and eat better by throwing the McDonald's supersized meal out and instead enjoying the luxury of dinner at a fine restaurant. How bad can that be?

If you're hesitant about cutting back on what you're eating, here are some easy ways to get started. When dining out, remember recommended serving sizes and visualize what one serving looks like. If you do that, you might think twice about eating that 8-ounce steak served at your favorite restaurant or the four slices of bread in that club sandwich. If you don't see anything on a restaurant's menu that might constitute a smaller portion, ask the waiter to wrap up half of your order before you finish eating—that way, you won't have overeaten and you will have another beautiful meal for the next day. You should also cancel your membership in the Clean Plate Club by leaving some food on your plate. To help maintain proper portion size, buy your meat from a butcher and ask him to cut it into 3-ounce portions. And be sure to buy the finest meat possible: you'll pay less for the highest-quality 3-ounce piece of meat than you would for a tough steak that weighs in at 8 ounces.

If the only change you make is cutting back on portion sizes, you would still make great progress toward better health. Start by reducing your food intake by just 10 percent: This small step alone could add five years to your life. Is it worth it? Let's say this change caused you to lose just 1 pound—this small weight loss will take 4 pounds of pressure off your knees. After you feel comfortable with your 10 percent daily calorie reduction, try making a few healthier food choices. Perhaps reduce the amount of bread you eat by eliminating it from one meal a day. Maybe eat fish for lunch or dinner—having a tuna sandwich instead of a hamburger would be a positive change. These choices are up to you, and they can even be a lot of fun. Just take a moment and make a plan. Just as you would when planning a trip, think about where you want to go and envision how you will enjoy the journey.

Keep a Food Diary

No matter how we much or how little we think we are eating, it's almost impossible to figure out exactly how much food you are putting into your body on a daily basis. That's why researchers at Kaiser Permanente Center for Health Research began tracking two thousand people who recorded in a food diary what they ate every day. What they found was that for every day that participants recorded what they ate, they lost weight. The process of writing down what you eat far surpasses exercise, age, or BMI as an indicator of weight gain or loss; the success of the Weight Watchers program can be partially attributed to food tracking.

Because many of us have no idea how much we are eating, it's not surprising that studies show that we underestimate by about 25 percent. We also tend to cut back on munching if we have to write down every Snickers bar we eat, every breath mint we put in our mouth, or every mocha latte we drink. By recording what we ingest, we also are forced to face the number of calories each swallow holds. It's a reality check that works like no other.

If you decide to keep a food diary, here are some tips on how to do it properly:

Choose how you're going to record your food: pen and paper, pre-organized book, online journal, or PDA.

» Record what you ate, how much, and when, and use measuring cups to monitor quantities.

» Tailor your chart to your own eating habits. Write down your personal hunger points, your cravings, when you ate, and how you were feeling.

» Be honest. Don't leave out anything, even a lick.

» Keep your diary close so you don't have to look for it whenever you need to write something down.

» At the end of the day, analyze what you ate and make healthy adjustments.

» Reward yourself! Treat yourself with a shopping trip or movie. Enjoy what you are doing for yourself.

"If you put a crouton on your sundae instead of a cherry, it counts as a salad."

DAILY FOOD DIARY

DATE_____

TIME: AM/PM

FOOD DESCRIPTION

AMOUNT IN OUNCES

FIBER IN GRAMS

TYPE OF BEVERAGE

AMOUNT IN OUNCES

_____

_____

_____

_____

_____

_____

_____

DAILY FOOD DIARY

DATE_____

TIME: AM/PM

FOOD DESCRIPTION

AMOUNT IN OUNCES

FIBER IN GRAMS

TYPE OF BEVERAGE

AMOUNT IN OUNCES

_____

_____

_____

_____

_____

_____

If you decided to go on a trip, you would never leave home without an idea of where you were going, so in the same vein, use your food diary as your road map on your journey to good health. Keeping a food diary may be the single most important thing you can do to stay on track.

Most importantly, it is crucial to change the way you think. For some reason, many of us feel the need to deprive ourselves because we don't think we deserve the best. But you deserve the best that good food has to offer. You have to believe that you can have a prime cut of meat, a fine glass of champagne, or a crystal bowl of berries. As the L'Oreal commercial tells us, "You're worth it."

TEN STEPS I AM TAKING ON MY JOURNEY TO GOOD HEALTH

Checked a food label to see how many calories were in a serving

Measured the amount of juice needed to fill my standard drinking glass

Put ½ cup of vegetables on a dinner plate

Cut out 4 ounces of soda today

Asked the butcher to cut a package of meat into 3-ounce servings

Took home half my main course from a favorite restaurant

Skipped bread with my dinner

Started a food diary

Served my iced tea in a champagne glass

Treated myself to a chocolate-dipped strawberry

The first wealth is health.

—Ralph Waldo Emerson

CHAPTER SIX

NUTRIENTS

Daily Rituals Are Important

Chapter 6: NUTRIENTS

Lifestyle changes cannot only extend the length of life but can also enhance the quality of life, particularly in our later years. Approximately 75 percent of the factors influencing life expectancy can be controlled, and one of the keys to good health is found in nutrients. While there are very valuable nutrients in the food you consume every day, supplements provide additional essential nutrients that are critically important to your health. Vitamins and minerals function as cofactors, or chemical helpers, in the chemical processes that occur every moment in every one of the ten trillion cells of your body. According to the *New England Journal of Medicine*, it is not only important that you eat right to achieve optimum health and nutrition, but you also need to take a multivitamin.

When we shop for healthy food, most of us rely on the manufacturer to provide us with ingredients that are good for us—however, I have researched hundreds of products and found that they fail to provide the percentage and/or quality of nutrients that we think we are getting when we make our purchases. We deserve better. Many of us are already trying to eat better, and we are taking the supplements we need for good health. For those with cancer, diabetes, high cholesterol, hypertension, and myriad other problems, taking supplements and eating properly may be lifesaving acts.

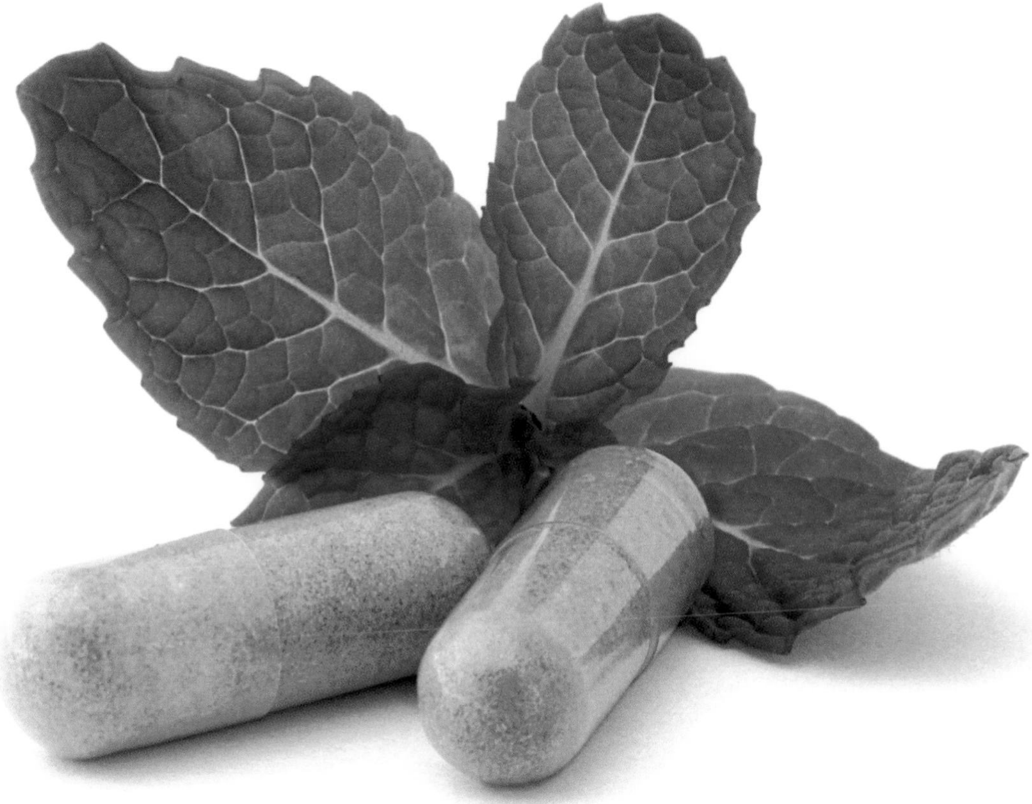

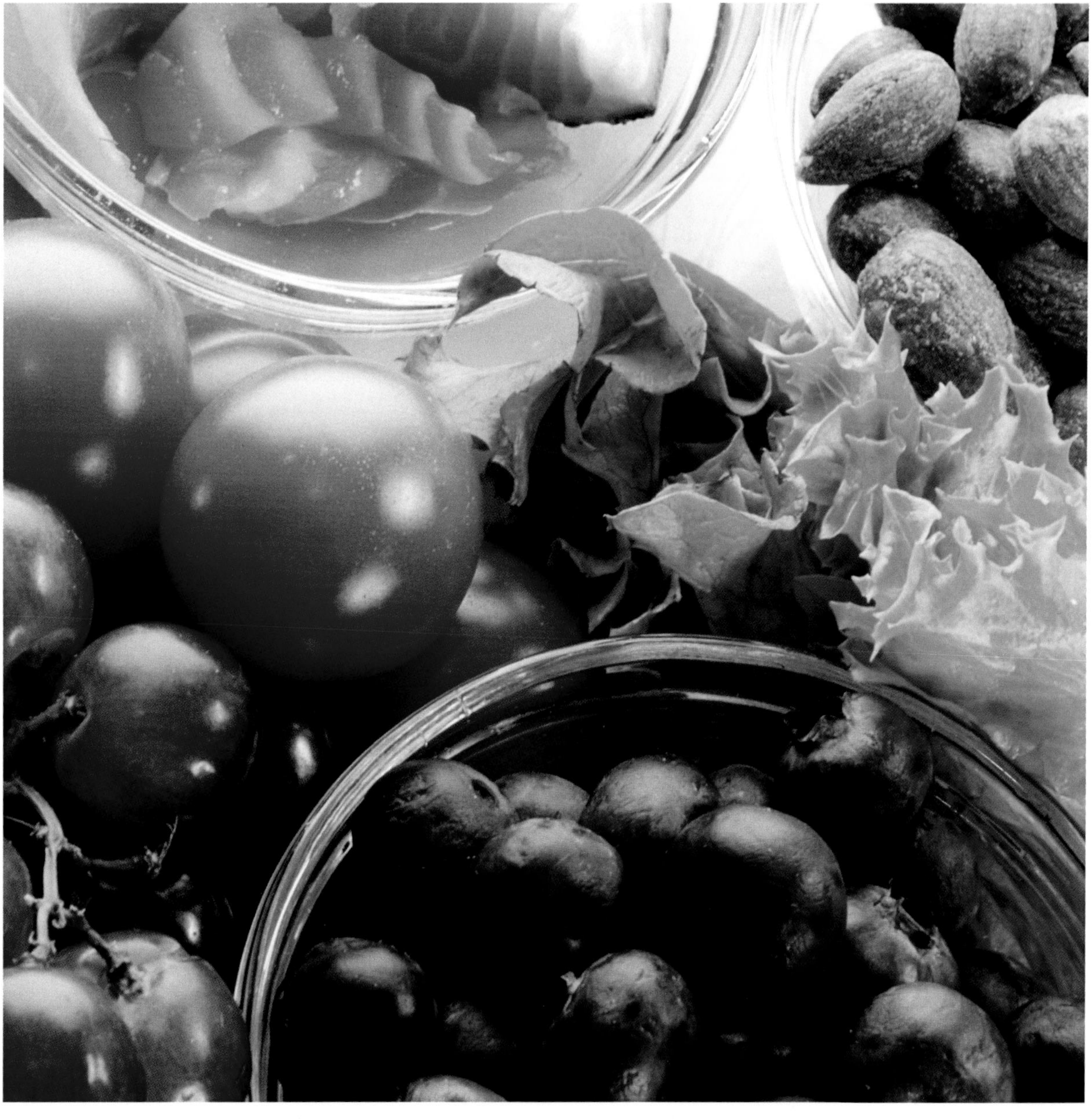

Four of the key nutrients that are important to monitor carefully are the following:

Antioxidants Vitamin D$_3$ Magnesium   Omega-3   Fatty Acids

Antioxidants

Antioxidants are critically involved in the prevention of damage to our cells. Antioxidant values are measured in Oxygen Radical Absorbance Capacity (ORAC); ORAC values represent the international testing standard developed by Dr. Guohua Cao, a physician and chemist at the National Institute on Aging in Baltimore, Maryland, and adopted by the USDA. The ORAC assay quantifies the ability of a material to effectively reduce oxidative stress. The best way to make sure you have the nutrients you need is to know the ORAC values of the food you eat—it is not the number of servings, but the value of the servings that counts.

ORAC Values for 3 Ounces (per 100 grams) of Common Foods

Dark Chocolate	13,120
Prunes	5,770
Raisins	2,830
Blueberries	2,400
Blackberries	2,036
Strawberries	1,540
Spinach, Raw	1,260
Broccoli Florets	890
Red Grapes	739
Cherries	670

Source: Data from U.S. Department of Agriculture and the *Journal of the American Chemical Society*

If you are like the average American, your intake of antioxidants probably is at around 1,200 ORAC a day. To be healthy, you need a minimum daily ORAC value of 3,000, while a daily ORAC value of up to 5,000 may be even better. Be very careful not to exceed a daily ORAC nutrient consumption because over this value antioxidants become pro-oxidants and this causes free radical damage to your cells. If you could do only one thing to improve your health and make it possible to live to be a healthy 120 years old, improve your antioxidant status. Longevity and a healthy life are dependent upon stopping free radical damage and supporting your cells' defense mechanisms with antioxidants. Just like an old piece of iron that has been left out in the environment, our cells break down due to oxidative damage caused by free radicals. We don't get old, we just rust out!

What Is a Free Radical?

Free radicals are chemical species produced by the cell's mitochondria as part of normal cellular respiration. Cells consist of many different types of molecules, that are in turn composed of atoms and electrons. Electrons are present in pairs, and free radicals have unpaired electrons. If unpaired, electrons seek others to pair with—molecules will attack other molecules to gain the needed electron. Free radicals are very unstable and react quickly in order to gain the required electron. When the "attacked" molecule loses its electron, it becomes a free radical itself and a chain reaction begins. Cellular damage can result. When free radicals react with other cellular components such as DNA, cells may die; causing real damage that could cause disease. It is important to note here that free radical damage can get worse as you get older.

When free radicals are overproduced, the body's natural antioxidant system defenses are weakened. The first result is oxidative stress, that then leads to oxidative injury and disease; heart disease and cancer are foremost among diseases caused by oxidative stress. Oxidative stress has also been seen as a secondary complication of many other diseases, including diabetes, arthritis, Parkinson's disease, and Alzheimer's disease, as well as aging.

Antioxidants Doing their Job

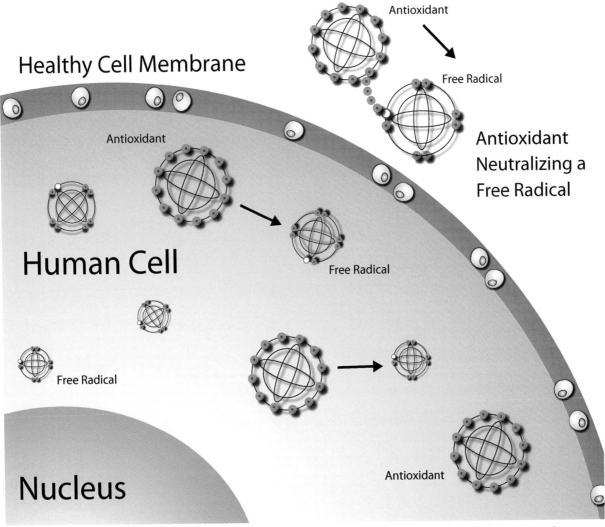

Antioxidant

Free Radical

Antioxidant Neutralizing a Free Radical

Healthy Cell Membrane

Antioxidant

Human Cell

Free Radical

Free Radical

Antioxidant

Nucleus

©McCord Research 2009

We don't get old, we just oxidize!

Antioxidants—molecules that can safely interact with free radicals to stop the chain reaction of cell damage—donate electrons to free radicals to stop their damaging effect. Antioxidants reverse the aging process and aid in preventing the onset of disease. The principal antioxidants involved are vitamin E, beta-carotene, and vitamin C. The body does not manufacture these nutrients, so they must come from nutrition or supplements. There is a delicate balance between oxidants and antioxidants in health and disease, and their proper balance is essential for ensuring healthy aging.

Although about one hundred million Americans are now using nutritional supplements that have antioxidant activity, there remains an urgent need to provide the general public with the most current information available about this important topic. Recent findings indicate that even genetic flaws can be corrected with vitamin and mineral supplements. Biomedical research to find specific genes that cause specific diseases will help identify enzymes in some people which will react better to supplements than others.

Olivamine®: A Combination of Antioxidants

For more than two hundred years researchers have studied the effects of nutrition on human health. The true dawning of nutritional research began in the early 1900s, and by the 1940s we were looking to nutritional science as a way to reduce disease associated with nutritional deficiencies. It was about this time that the Recommended Daily Allowance (RDA) for nutrients was established.

Today the focus in nutritional research has changed: now we are looking at how the nutrients we consume affect our genes. The field of research that studies the effects of nutrients on our genes is called nutrigenomics. This emerging area of research is considered by many to be the next important frontier of medicine—it provides the vital link between longevity and reduction of all major diseases, and the use of high-tech research in the fight to improve quality of life without prescription drugs. The stakes are high—and the rewards are even higher.

Olivamine is a proprietary trade secret formula that is based in nutrigenomic research. Ingredients found in this one-of-a-kind formula provide patients with the opportunity to change the course of so-called normal aging and the diseases associated with it, thus leading to a longer and healthier life. It is generally recognized that most human diseases are largely avoidable with lifestyle changes, and emerging Olivamine research will aid in the understanding of how nutrients can positively affect the risk of cancer, other chronic diseases, and aging—and this places nutrigenomics at the forefront of preventive medicine.

The Olivamine formula is composed of seven small molecules, each with the proven ability to extend the life of aged and diseased cells or to serve as co-factors that make the processes possible. The amino acid N-acetyl-L-cysteine (NAC) is proven to protect the mitochondria and thus assist in cell survival. NAC protects aging and damaged cells when normal processes have otherwise failed. In published research conducted at The University of Iowa, the role of NAC in the survival of cells has been examined. NAC significantly improves cell survival. Its role is critical in reducing the effects of disease and aging associated with free radical damage.

The phytochemical hydroxytyrosol has been proven to activate the FOX03a protein, known to improve longevity and reduce the risks of disease. While scientists are just beginning to unlock the secrets of this important protein, what is known now is that if this protein is off (i.e., not activated), the cellular processes that extend life and fight diseases such as breast cancer are also not working. The FOX03a protein may then hold the promise of extending lives and maintaining healthy cells that will survive when without treatment would die.

In a study in the April 16, 2008, issue of the journal *Cell*, it was reported that when activated, the FOX03a protein acted as a tumor suppressor, particularly in breast cancer patients. Research conducted at University of Texas's M. D. Anderson Cancer Center and published in *Cell* showed that the activation of the FOX03a protein is associated with better outcomes for cancer patients. Researchers examined the role of FOX03a in tumor cells of 131 breast cancer patients. When they looked at patient survival they found a strong correlation between active FOX03a and better survival rates. Additional research revealed the FOX03a protein was found in patients with stomach, liver, and lung cancer and may hold promise for better treatment protocols for patients with these cancers. Hydroxytyrosol is the main component of Olivamine and it has been proven in research to activate FOX03a. Further research is being conducted at Iowa to determine the role of hydroxytyrosol in improved aging and cancer outcomes.

In addition, Olivamine contains important B vitamins that act as "keys" to make other ingredients bioavailable to our bodies. These vitamins, B_3 and B_6, serve as co-factors for the amino acids found in the formula—in addition to NAC, these amino acids are glycine, L-Proline, and L-Taurine. Vitamins B_3 and B_6 are vital nutrients to our overall health, and they additionally ensure the activity of Olivamine. Each of the amino acids in Olivamine provides vital support for aged cells. Finally, Olivamine contains methylsulfonylmethane (MSM), a necessary ingredient in our bodies that protects our joints against aging.

While Olivamine can only be found in this author's products, that is not really the point: the point to be made here is that I am really interested in saving lives. A lot of important research has gone into the formulation of Olivamine and the ingredients found in it. And truly, I find them to be life changing, if not life saving.

Olivamine was first available in topical form in a line of skin care products that I developed. These products are sold under the Remedy label and are the best-selling line sold in this nation's hospitals, nursing homes, and long-term care facilities. Within just a few years, my skin and wound care products became the brand leader in a highly competitive market. The product's success came because my products simply outperform the competition.

The value of Olivamine in skin and wound care has been demonstrated for the treatment of the most severe skin diseases when used topically. And Olivamine is now available in McCord Research's Pinnaclife® Supplements, taken orally. By taking Olivamine as part of a supplement regimen, every cell in your body can benefit from its renewing effects.

One of the most important aspects of Olivamine is the ability of hydroxytyrosol and NAC, two of the formula's key ingredients, to reverse extended cellular quiescence (abnormal cellular resting without dividing). As we age, cells tend to slow down and stay quiescent (in a resting status) for extended periods of time; many of these cells then die without participating in cell and organ renewal.

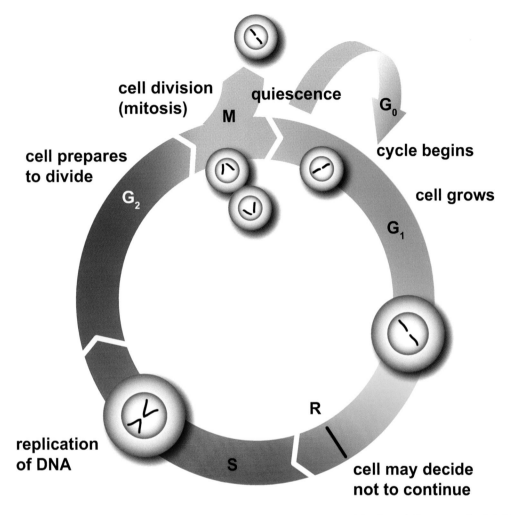

cell division
(mitosis)

quiescence

cell prepares
to divide

G_2

M

G_0

cycle begins

cell grows

G_1

R

replication
of DNA

S

cell may decide
not to continue

©McCord Research 2009

Hydroxytyrosol and NAC have been shown to cause cells in extended quiescence to return to the cell cycle. This is one of the keys to antiaging, or in other words, finding the much-sought-after "Fountain of Youth."

Total Antioxidant Capacity of Fruits

Expressed as micromole Trolox equivalent per gram (TE/g) dry mass (DM)

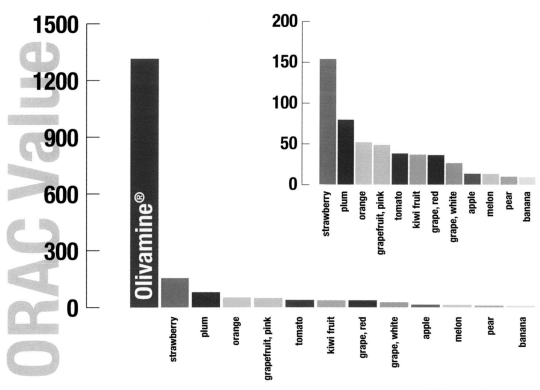

©McCord Research 2009

Total Antioxidant Capacity of Vegtables

Expressed as micromole Trolox equivalent per gram (TE/g) dry mass (DM)

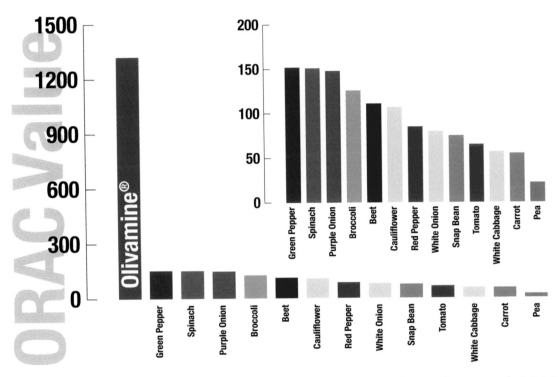

©McCord Research 2009

The ability of a material to effectively reduce oxidative stress is determined by the ORAC assay method. Olivamine has been tested to determine its ORAC value as compared to fruits and vegetables known for their antioxidant activity. Brunswick Laboratories conducted the testing utilizing the Cobas Fara II centrifugal analyzer.

Vitamin D$_3$

The evidence is overwhelming that we are deficient in vitamin D$_3$—in fact, more than $560 billion has been spent by Medicare alone to treat diseases linked to vitamin D$_3$ deficiency. Studies have shown that conditions as diverse as cancer, diabetes, and bone disease are linked to this deficiency. Most of us are aware of the role vitamin D$_3$ plays in bone health—but in order to make a difference in your body you need at least 1,000 IU of this vitamin each day. The FDA and the USDA currently recommend only 400 IU as the standard daily requirement, but most research scientists working in the field believe that these organizations will see the error in this because the science for that standard is outdated. In fact, recent research has shown that vitamin D$_3$ deficiency is extremely common, further suggesting that our current recommended daily dosage is too low. (If you have had breast or prostate cancer or are concerned about these cancers, your daily intake may need to be as high as 2,000 IU per day.)

The human body produces vitamin D when exposed to sunshine; forms of vitamin D can also be found in some foods, including salmon, some dairy products, and fortified cereals.

I'll wager that when you purchased your last half gallon of fortified milk, you thought that the form of vitamin D added to it was D$_3$, the one vital for good health—however, unless you purchased organic milk you most likely got the cheaper form of vitamin D, vitamin D$_2$, a form that is of little or no value to you.

As noted above, researchers and physicians alike are working with the federal government to get the recommended daily requirement for vitamin D$_3$ increased from 400 IU to 1,000 IU, a move that could likely save hundreds of thousands of lives each year. In controlled scientific studies designed to evaluate the effectiveness of vitamin D$_3$ against cancer, vitamin D$_3$ was shown to affect more than two hundred genes responsible for regulating cell proliferation (uncontrolled cell division), differentiation (defining features), and apoptosis (natural cell death). Without adequate vitamin D$_3$, the critical balance between these processes is lost, and the risk of many forms of cancer is nearly doubled. When the regulatory genes lack the vitamin D necessary to maintain the balance of apoptosis, proliferation, and differentiation, cancer cells have the opportunity to take hold.

1,000 IU of Vitamin D_3 Reduces the Risk of Cancer

Type of Cancer	Reduction to Risk with D_3
Breast	50 percent
Colon	50 percent
Ovarian	36 percent
Prostate	49 percent

In research reported in the *New England Journal of Medicine*, deficient levels of vitamin D_3 were found to be a major contributor to disease, as indicated below; it also showed that the addition of vitamin D_3 in the amounts indicated substantially reduced the risk.

Disease	Percent Change	Dose
Multiple Sclerosis (in women)	42 percent reduction	400 IU daily
Type 2 Diabetes	33 percent reduction	800 IU Daily + calcium

The researchers went on to report that there is a correlation between increased incidences of many diseases in people with low vitamin D_3 levels, including:

Autoimmune diseases	Cardiovascular diseases
Depression	Hypertension
Osteoarthritis	Pulmonary disorders
Schizophrenia	

In an article titled "The Urgent Need to Recommend an Intake of Vitamin D that Is Effective" that was published in the American Journal of Clinical Nutrition, the authors are critical of the government for not warning the public of the health risks associated with of vitamin D_3 levels below 30 ng/mL.

As we struggle with out-of-control health costs, it is crucial to inform people about reducing their risk of disease by simply adding a low-cost supplement to their diet. Not only could such a simple action save millions of lives each year, but also it could save billions of taxpayer dollars. Nontoxic vitamin D_3 is safe and effective in the prevention of diseases. So what are we waiting for?

Vitamin D is actually a hormone, and the natural source of vitamin D is the sun—we evolved with sunlight. However, over the past few decades we have been led to believe that the sun is our enemy, and so we've spent billions of dollars on sunscreens that block sunlight's healing benefits. Even as industry has put sunscreens in everything from makeup to shampoos, they have failed to mention one correlation: skin cancer cases have increased in direct proportion to the use of sunscreens. The fact is, you need sunlight every day: without it, your risk of serious diseases is increased substantially.

A healthy relationship with the sun will allow us to reduce our risks of many diseases and save a lot of money on these sunscreen products, that contain toxic chemicals. It only takes a few minutes of exposure to sunlight a day if you live in the southern half of the United States. If you live in the northern part of the country, you will need to supplement with vitamin D_3.

Top Ten Sources of Dietary Vitamin D

Food	Weight	Milligrams (mg)	%DV
Cod liver oil	1 tablespoon	1,360	340
Salmon, cooked	3.5 ounces	360	90
Mackerel, cooked	3.5 ounces	345	90
Tuna, canned in oil	3 ounces	200	50
Sardines, canned in oil, drained	1.75 ounces	250	70
Milk, nonfat, reduced fat, and hole, vitamin D-fortified	1 cup★	98	25
Margarine, fortified,	1 tablespoon	60	15
Egg	1 whole (vitamin D is found in yolk)	20	6
Liver, beef, cooked	3.5 ounces	15	4
Cheese, Swiss	1 ounce	12	4

★ May be in the form of D_2 and not D_3 as needed—check the label and do not count if D_2 has been added.

Magnesium

Magnesium regulates more than 325 enzymes in the body that produce, transport, and store cellular energy—it is indispensable to life. DNA and RNA synthesis, cell growth, and cell reproduction are all regulated by magnesium. Magnesium orchestrates the "electric current" that causes our nerves to respond properly, and without it our muscle and nerve functions are compromised. Reduced magnesium may be responsible for or be involved with:

Anxiety	Arrhythmia
Constipation	Depression
Fatigue	Hypertension
Kidney disease	Leg cramps
Muscular weakness	Seizures
Tooth decay	Weak bones

We all know about the benefits of calcium, but did you know that calcium enters the cell through ports known as calcium channels and that these channels are "guarded" by magnesium? Magnesium concentrations in cells are ten thousand times greater than those of calcium, and magnesium allows only a certain amount of calcium to enter cells: magnesium is our body's natural calcium channel blocker, and without magnesium, calcium cannot work properly. When you take too much calcium, it is almost impossible to get enough magnesium to correct the imbalance. Within the ancient diet there was a ratio of 1:1 calcium to magnesium—today that ratio is somewhere between 5:1 to 15:1. When you take supplements, look for one that provides more magnesium than calcium to help overcome this imbalance. Because our brains are "electrically charged" and we need magnesium to keep brain cells powered up as we age, it may be said, "Get smart: Take magnesium!"

Your very life is dependent on magnesium: in fact, without magnesium there simply is no life; it is that simple. So how and why have so many of us become deficient in magnesium? One of the main reasons is our diet, not only what we eat but what is missing from our food after processing. Not only is the soil in which our food is grown depleted of magnesium, but what little may be left is often destroyed as food is processed.

Top Ten Sources of Dietary Magnesium

Food	Weight	Milligrams (mg)	%DV
Halibut, cooked	3 ounces	90	20
Almonds, dry roasted	1 ounce	80	20
Cashews, dry roasted	1 ounce	75	20
Soybeans, mature, cooked	½ cup	75	20
Spinach, frozen, cooked	½ cup	75	20
Nuts, mixed, dry roasted	1 ounce	65	15
Cereal, shredded wheat	2 rectangular biscuits	55	15
Oatmeal, instant, fortified, prepared w/water	1 cup	55	15
Potato, baked w/skin	1 medium	50	15
Peanuts, dry roasted	1 ounce	50	15

Omega-3 Fatty Acids

A lipid membrane covers every cell of your body. When a cell is damaged by free radicals it is this protective lipid membrane that is first to be compromised; if not repaired, the cell will die prematurely. Talk about a formula for early aging! More important, the greatest numbers of "fatty" cells in your body are found in your brain—this is why mental health and neurological wellness are often associated with omega-3 fatty acid intake. Omega-3 essential fatty acids play a crucial role in brain function as well as normal growth and development. (The word "essential" is used in front of "fatty acid" to denote that it is essential to total health, but the body does not produce the nutrient and it must be supplied through diet and supplements.) Research has shown that omega-3 fatty acids are the "brain food" that keeps the neural networks functioning at high levels, improving memory and behavior. Not only can they affect your brain performance, but they also impact mood and depression—fatigue, poor memory, and mood swings are in fact often symptoms of an omega-3 fatty acid deficiency.

The body uses three types of omega-3 fatty acids: alpha-linolenic acid (ALA), eicosapentaenoic acid (EPA), and docosahexaenoic acid (DHA). Once consumed, ALA is converted in our bodies to EPA and DHA. While a diet rich in oily fish such as mackerel, tuna, and salmon—walnuts are another good source—is important to maintain good health, the addition of omega-3 fatty acids in a supplemental form is essential. Because of the possible mercury content in fatty fish such as swordfish, shark, and king mackerel, it is recommended that you take dietary supplements that are certified as being mercury free.

There are two major classes of polyunsaturated fatty acids (PUFAs): omega-3 and omega-6 fatty acids. While there is scientific evidence that individuals should consume more omega-3 and fewer omega-6 fatty acids for good health, most American diets provide at least ten times more omega-6 fatty acids than omega-3 fatty acids. Only 25 percent of the population reported consuming enough daily omega-3 fatty acids.

The essential fatty acids that we need to supplement in our diets are ALA and linoleic acid (LA), because the body cannot make them.

ALA is present in leafy green vegetables, nuts, vegetable oils (such as canola), and especially in flaxseed and flaxseed oil. Good sources of omega-3 are fish (both finfish and shellfish and their oils and eggs) and organ meats. LA is found in many foods consumed by Americans, including meat and vegetable oils (safflower, canola, sunflower, corn, and soy).

Omega-3 Fatty Acids for Cardiovascular Health and Disease Prevention

Epidemiological studies first published in the late 1970s noted relatively low cardiovascular mortality in populations (such as Eskimos) that reported high fish consumption. The apparent health benefits of fish are explained, at least in part, by the EPA and DHA (found in omega-3 sources) they contain. Since these early studies, hundreds of observational and clinical trials have been conducted to evaluate the effects of EPA and DHA from marine sources and ALA from plant sources on cardiovascular disease and its many risk factors and intermediate markers. Studies have also sought to understand the potential benefits of increased intakes of omega-3 fatty acids.

According to the NIH, there is evidence from both primary and secondary prevention studies to support the hypothesis that consumption of omega-3 fatty acids (found in fish and fish oil) reduces all-cause mortality and various cardiovascular outcomes such as sudden death, cardiac death, and myocardial infarction (heart attack). The evidence is strongest for fish or fish oil: the potential effects of ALA are largely unknown and the relative effects of ALA versus fish oil are not well defined. In the only randomized clinical trial (RCT) that directly compared ALA and fish oil, both treatments reduced cardiovascular disease (CVD) outcome.

Furthermore, strong evidence shows that fish-oil supplements had a substantial and beneficial effect on triglycerides, that increased with larger intakes of fish oil: most studies reported a net decrease of triglycerides of about 10 to 33 percent. There is also evidence of a very small beneficial effect of fish oils on blood pressure as well as possible positive effects on coronary artery restenosis (recurrence of artery blockage) after angioplasty, exercise capacity in patients with coronary atherosclerosis (narrowing or hardening of the arteries), and heart rate variability (particularly in patients with recent myocardial infarctions).

	Amount per serving	% Daily Value
Vitamin C (ascorbic acid)	100 mg	16%
Potassium (from glucosamine sulfate KCl)	61 mg	2%
Chloride (from glucosamine sulfate KCl)	56 mg	2%
Glucosamine sulfate KCl	500 mg	†
Supplying sulfur 80 mg		
MSM	1 gram (1000 mg)	
Supplying sulfur 340mg		

* Percent Daily Value is based on a 2000 calorie diet.
† Daily Value not established.

Other ingredients: cellulose, magnesium stearate (vegetable source), gelatin capsule.

How to Read a Supplement Label

Understanding the back of a supplement bottle can be as easy as 1-2-3, but you have to know what you're reading. There are two ways in which labels are often written that are not helpful. First, if you pick up a supplement bottle and see listings of vitamins and minerals and underneath that list is the technical name for all those vitamins, that's the worst possible scenario: that indicates a manufacturer who really doesn't want you to know what you're taking.

If a label lists a vitamin with its description—i.e., the legal description of what you are taking (see photo at left)—this is helpful information. If a manufacturer's label is not disclosing to you what you are taking, then put that bottle down and buy from a company that wants you to know and understand what is in their product.

You also have to choose between capsules and tablets. Tablets are filled with binders, fillers, and other unnecessary ingredients; capsules, which are more expensive to produce, are not. While capsules may be more costly, you don't have to worry about the pills breaking apart by the time they reach your stomach, and capsules can be color-coded to make identifying your supplements easy.

Taking Supplements as a Ritual

There is much scientific data that tells us that a healthy diet should include a daily supplement regimen. I like to call this regimen a ritual: this routine is a practice that is life affirming, and we need to embrace it and make it a daily habit. It is simple and painless, and it can save your life if you do it properly.

The science behind certain nutrient supplements can perhaps be difficult to grasp, but it is imperative that you know what key ingredients constitute a good nutrient plan so that you can choose wisely which one to make part of your daily ritual. My goal is to keep you on the journey to good health and longevity: You have the choice to take the steps necessary to fulfill that goal. Something as simple as adding a daily supplement ritual may change your life.

This one step—choosing a goal and staying to it—changes everything.
—Scott Reed

TEN STEPS I AM TAKING ON MY JOURNEY TO GOOD HEALTH

Got a blood test to know my vitamin and mineral status

Started on a good supplement program

Examined my current supplement label to make sure it was "good"

Ate foods that were high in antioxidants

Got out into the sun for twenty minutes to help my vitamin D status

Ate a handful of nuts for good health

Examined my diet to make sure I was getting key nutrients

Realized that good health was due to my lifestyle choices

Ate a tuna sandwich for lunch instead of a hamburger

Ate salmon for dinner

A good laugh and a long sleep are the best cures in the doctor's book.

—Irish Proverb

CHAPTER SEVEN
EMOTIONAL HEALTH

Leave Stress Behind

Chapter 7: Emotional Health

It should come as no surprise to anyone that emotional well-being is linked with physical health. Stress hormones, when released over a continuous period of time, have been shown to directly impact cardiovascular disease. But it is not just heart disease that has found to be affected by stress: If you're happy, stress-free, and relaxed, you're less likely to suffer from serious conditions such as diabetes and cancer, as well as relatively minor problems such as fatigue, upset stomach, and even the common cold. The bad news is that stress is on the rise.

According to the American Psychological Association, 48 percent of those surveyed in a recent study reported that their stress levels had increased over the last five years. The good news is that we now have more tools than ever to deal with stress. Scientists are conducting numerous studies on how to measure what's going on in the brain and now claim that optimism and happiness are no longer as elusive as they once were. While it is believed that genetic factors contribute one-third towards our attitude, the rest is up to us. If we choose to be happy in our daily lives, most likely we will be healthier as well. As we make our way on our journey to good health and a long life, let's consider our trip a relaxing and carefree vacation. According to experts, optimists tend to experience stressors differently and adapt better to healthy lifestyles; these things lead to a healthier immune system. Among recent

major research findings is that happy people are not only healthier and live longer, but they also are more productive at work, have better relationships, and are generally more well-liked.

Although it's very hard to define what happiness is for each individual, most people generally agree that it involves the sense that your life is good, meaningful, and engaging. It is the feeling that you are doing something so engrossing that you lose all track of time, whether it's listening to a beautiful song, taking a walk on the beach, or holding a yoga pose. It also comes from such meaningful activities as engaging in mental exercises that sharpen your brain or volunteering a few hours at your local animal shelter or church. Something as simple as donating a toy to a local charity involves you in a cause greater than yourself, that experts have said is a key component to attaining emotional well-being.

Change can be as simple as adopting a positive mental attitude. In our busy lives, we are often bothered by negative self-talk: Was I productive enough? Did I eat all the right things? Did I get enough exercise? What if I failed to do what I set out to do? Instead of focusing on what you didn't accomplish, express gratitude for what is available to you today. That's why we focus on milestones. And every small step in our journey is a milestone.

Most of us are driven by different forces, including competition, seeking approval, old beliefs, guilt, or even fear. How we live our lives depends on how these steer our daily activities and attitudes. If we let go of these often destructive forces and stop listening to the scolding voices in our heads, we can make room for positive change and stress-free lives. Every time you relax and let go of something that you thought you had to do, you are on your way to a healthier and longer life.

The changes we suggest are often so simple that you probably won't even notice that you've stopped years of aging with almost no effort. Small changes may be the most meaningful, and the most basic ones are surprisingly effective. And even if you don't succeed in changing something today, just acknowledging that you would like to change is a major step.

Just Sit There and Savor the Moment

Simply doing nothing can be a positive change in your life. If you have a tendency to run around and constantly do things, sit down and allow time to hear yourself think. Give yourself a day to go somewhere peaceful: go to the beach or take a hike. Find your favorite beautiful spot and bring along a picnic—and if it's chilly, don't forget the marshmallows! Remember, you can also enjoy a beautiful sunrise or sunset, that costs the same for the billionaire as for the person with no money at all. You need to get back to the basics and remember this old adage: "The best things in life are free."

The first step toward change is acceptance. Once you accept yourself, you open the door to change. That's all you have to do. Change is not something you do, it is something you allow.

—Will Garcia

Losing yourself in a sunset as you sip a glass of wine may be your personal form of meditation. "Yoga" and "meditation" are scary words for many people, but you don't have to be a guru to practice either one. It's not necessary to assume the lotus position, sit absolutely still, and think of nothing for ten hours. Meditation, loosely defined, is a clearing of the mind—let everything from your busy day go and listen to your favorite relaxing music. As you focus on the music, you can begin to hear and feel the notes and allow the notes to come into your life. You can also practice something as simple as breathing in and out three times a day. The practice of meditation is one that simply allows your mind to be at rest and be peaceful. Try to find a spot you find peaceful, be it your bathtub, in front of the fireplace, or among a grove of pine trees. The purpose is to get in touch with yourself or with nature and the universe and allow all the problems of your day to melt away.

Meditation: Another Word for Relaxation

The word "meditation" may conjure up a vision of a bearded man sitting cross-legged atop a high mountain. If that image is the one you associate with meditation, try using the word "relaxation" instead. The idea is to get rid of all "chatter" in our heads that constantly takes us away from a peaceful state. Focusing on our breathing is one way of letting go of those busy internal voices. Just closing your eyes and listening to music can be a form of meditation.

At Massachusetts General Hospital, Dr. Randall Zusman used a "relaxation response" technique to lower blood pressure in forty of the sixty patients in a controlled study. The technique Dr. Zusman taught his patients consisted of sitting quietly for ten to twenty minutes and repeating a word while focusing on breathing. At the end of the study patients were able to eliminate daily blood pressure medication within a few months. Many of them had been doubtful that such a technique would work, but in the end they experienced significant results. Zusman based his studies on a technique first recognized more than thirty years ago by cardiologist Robert Benson. With additional science to back it up today, the relaxation response has been found to increase the formation of nitric oxide; a compound that opens up the blood vessels and in turn lowers blood pressure.

Here's one way you can practice meditation with a very simple relaxation technique: Breathe in through your nose to a count of four and say to yourself, "I am"; breathe out from the bottom of your stomach and exhale through your mouth, repeating or thinking the word "calm." Fill your lungs with fresh air. As you exhale, think of a word that brings you peace—practice with different words, such as "joy," "calm," or "serenity." When you breathe in and out, you are letting the negative and positive energy move about your body and out in the space around you. You can bring in joy and happiness and let out anger and frustration in a simple exchange of one type of energy for another. What a great thing to do on a plane . . .

Even though Dr. Zusman's study involved setting aside a specific period of time each day to relax and focus on breathing, if you can just imagine the difference that slowing down can make, you have taken another important step toward finding the Fountain of Youth.

The Importance of Sleep

One-third of our lives is spent sleeping, and that time spent can be as critical to good health as the things we do when we are awake. Because our bodies need time to rest and regenerate, seven to eight hours of sleep can lead to a more productive and enjoyable life. And good sleep can add three to five years to your life.

The best way to get a good night's sleep is to clear your mind. The thoughts that keep running through your mind when you are trying to go to sleep—paying the bills, getting certain things done, going over the bad events of the day, worrying about what's coming up—can lead to long, restless nights that are completely unproductive and even harmful to you. If you have a stress point that is causing you to lose sleep, it is important to recognize it and try to eliminate it from your life.

Approximately one out of three Americans experiences sleep problems. That's why scientists have taken a serious interest in sleep disorders. Although researchers disagree on the exact connections between sleep patterns and health problems, several studies have shown that lack of sleep can affect such conditions as obesity, heart attacks and strokes, diabetes, and some forms of cancer. Sleep deprivation has also led to more traffic accidents and even death from people falling asleep at the wheel. In addition, sleep apnea—a common disorder where airways become blocked during sleep, causing short periods where breathing actually stops—has become widely diagnosed. There's no doubt that good-quality sleep is linked to longevity, while disruptive sleep has been shown to be an indication of faster aging. Most people need seven to nine hours of sleep, and there is apparently an increased risk for disease when people get fewer than six hours of sleep on a regular basis. Sleep deficits can increase the production of stress hormones, which in turn drives up blood pressure; it also causes the production of substances in the blood that cause inflammation in the body, predisposing people to shortened life spans.

Sleep can also contribute to the regulation of our appetites by regulating the balance of the hormones ghrelin and leptin, which are involved in determining our levels of hunger or fullness. Thus, sleep can even contribute to weight control.

It may be difficult to clear your mind before going to sleep, but you may want to try these ten tips to better sleep:

- » Listen to restful, soothing music and get lost in the notes while letting go of the day's activity.
- » Take a warm, fragrant bath ninety minutes before bedtime in a dimly lit bathroom.
- » Drink a cup of herbal tea in a fine china teacup.
- » Get into a routine before you go to bed. Make sleep a ritual.
- » Don't go to bed until you are sleepy; reduce the time spent lying awake in bed.
- » Make sure all of the lights are turned out.
- » Try to go to bed at the same time each night.
- » Don't drink stimulants such as coffee (even decaffeinated), tea, or alcohol before you go to sleep. You can drink herbal tea instead, and perhaps eat a light snack to keep you from getting hungry during the night.
- » Refrain from vigorous exercise several hours before going to bed.
- » Get out of bed if you can't go to sleep within twenty minutes. Try to do something relaxing before going back to bed.

As for daytime naps, a recent study showed that those who took regular midday "cat" naps of about thirty minutes at least three times a week had a 37 percent reduction in their risk of dying from a heart-related problem. Studies show that, especially for men, a short nap can help relieve the stresses of the day. However, if you are having trouble sleeping at night, try to avoid taking naps—it is always better to get your sleep at night.

Before going to bed or perhaps at some point during the night, you may hear a nagging voice in your head that reminds you about something, perhaps, for example, that your car is getting low on gas and that you need to fill it up right now. Tell yourself that for the next eight hours there isn't a gas station around, so there's absolutely nothing you can do about it. Remember that worrying doesn't help at all. Let your troubles go for now, and rest assured that you will be reminded of them in the morning.

The Importance of Laughter

The sound of laughter is far more contagious than any disease. It is commonly accepted that laughter can decrease stress, lower blood pressure, increase brain function, and improve immune function. It does this by reducing the production of stress hormones such as cortisol, epinephrine (adrenaline), and dopamine, as well as increasing the production of healthy hormones such as endorphins. Laughter can actually enhance the effectiveness of T-cells, those cells that help to suppress destructive cells, and it can activate the autoimmune system, allowing us to fight off the effects of stress. Isn't it hard to laugh and be angry at the same time?

Laughter is also a form of physical exercise that involves moving your abdomen, diaphragm and shoulders, and breathing deeply. A good belly laugh exercises your body like no other form of movement. It can exercise up to fifteen different facial muscles, as well as others throughout your body, by causing them to flex and relax. Laughter stimulates the cardiovascular system and increases blood flow.

Laughter may be a way of doing sit-ups for the soul . . . or how about thinking about it as internal jogging? According to Lee Berk, clinical researcher at Loma Linda University, "The biological changes we see with constant routine exercise are very similar to the changes we see with constant use of mirthful laughter." Ten to fifteen minutes of daily

Laughter Is the Best Medicine. Nobody ever died of laughter.

—Max Beerbohm

laughter can be equal to ten minutes on the rowing machine. Among its other benefits, laughter has been shown to suppress appetite, eliminate boredom and depression, and keep your mind off the refrigerator. Even more interesting, studies have shown that it doesn't even matter if you are faking laughter—you can still achieve positive results.

Laughing at yourself can put any problem into perspective by making you realize that it's not as earth-shattering as you thought. It also helps release pent-up frustrations and angers. Laughter connects us to each other: we talk more, touch each other more, and get through hard times together better.

Laughter is now being taught in the workplace: experts on laughter and how to play are being hired to teach adults how to reconnect with the playful child in all of us. Laughter is a tool that not only helps to stimulate interpersonal relationships, but also provides a necessary release from the stresses involved in many jobs. If you have trouble bringing laughter into your life, there are humor therapists and laughter therapists who can help you. Even laughter yoga, which combines breathing and laughter, has gained attention throughout the world; it is based on the simple concept that laughter brings more oxygen to the body and brain, thus creating physiological as well as psychological benefits.

Children are good role models for taking life more lightly. We can emulate their behavior in many ways, from telling silly jokes to making funny faces to playing with toys. We all need to take life less seriously and try to incorporate humor into our everyday lives.

Here are a few ways that we can enjoy the benefits that laughter provides:

» When you hear people laughing, move toward them.

» Try to be less serious and laugh at yourself more often.

» Watch comedy DVDs and TV shows. Don't forget classics such as *I Love Lucy*, movies starring the Marx Brothers, or shows featuring memorable comedians such as Jack Benny or George Burns and Gracie Allen.

» Have a "Comedy Night" one night a week at home: Rent a classic comedy DVD or simply watch Comedy Central on cable.

» Read comic books and joke books. Check out authors who write humor.

» Go to a comedy club.

» Hang out with friends who make you laugh. Play games such as charades or Pictionary. Make a simple get-together a party.

» Try to see the humor in everyday life instead of complaining about it. Look back at situations that were difficult and retell them to friends in a humorous way.

» Since fake laughter can be as useful as real laughter, try a few belly laughs in front of the mirror.

» Remember a silly joke someone told you and repeat it to a friend.

Use Your Mind

Learning is a lifetime process, one that shouldn't stop just because you are out of school. Mental exercise is the best way to prevent conditions such as Alzheimer's disease and dementia. Learning forces you to grow new connections to nerve cells, and there's no time like the present to learn how to do something new. Follow a new recipe, start a vegetable garden, take piano lessons, or simply do a *New York Times* crossword puzzle: all of these activities help stimulate significant information processing. As your mind grows more active, so does your body.

It is important to know that aging does not necessarily bring on decreased mental function. All of us have little lapses in memory, like leaving a key in the door or forgetting to bring your grocery list to the market. Usually these "brain blips" are caused by stress or lack of concentration. Aging does not necessarily limit mental capacity. In older people, even small amounts of mental stimulation or mental "exercise" can improve brain function. The National Institute of Aging has conducted studies that show that most dramatic memory loss occurs around age seventy (if at all). And even if your memory fades, your thinking ability does not. Vocabulary and reasoning skills can even improve with age.

In your local public library you can most likely find a book or DVD from the Teaching Company; in these materials you can learn from the greatest professors in the world. This excellent resource features the top one hundred lecturers speaking on every possible subject, from history

to quantum physics: With these resources, it's as if you are attending the most prestigious university in the world in the comfort of your own home. Your television can also be a source of fascinating information if you tune in to such channels as the Discovery Channel, the History Channel, or National Geographic.

If you prefer a more social form of learning, take a course from your local college or university, or attend an evening Extension class. Some schools offer what they call "senior college" for those who want to spend their retirement years expanding their minds with newfound knowledge, a surefire antidote to boredom, fatigue, or even mental disease. If you don't have time to enroll in a full course, you could pick up that calendar that teaches a different fact every day, or perhaps pick up a dictionary and learn a new word every day. Other simple activities can stimulate learning: take a different route to your favorite restaurant or visit your local art museum; take up that hobby that you always wanted to do but never had time for, whether cooking, woodworking, scrapbooking, or learning how to use the computer.

While many of you have probably seen the book *1000 Places to See Before You Die*, remember that you don't have to travel to faraway locales: make a list of ten places in your local area that you can visit at least once this year. You can refer to your local newspaper for ideas, or consider the following list:

Museum	Zoo
Aquarium	Arboretum or botanical garden
State or national park	State or county fair
Theater	Concert
Historic site, building, or monument	College campus

As you travel to that favorite spot, whether it's located in your neighborhood or outside your city, you can enjoy your journey by listening to a CD in the car—perhaps great music,

an interesting lecture, or a recorded book. All of us spend so much time in our cars, and we should see this time as a great opportunity to relax or even improve our lives as we travel along. You can use your car as a place to find solitude or peace, especially if you choose to listen to your favorite music. Or you can make it your goal to listen to one great book a month in your car.

Whatever you do, make sure it's fun. If you're too tired to go out, stay home and learn a new game: Get the new international version of Monopoly, play video poker on the Internet, or learn how to play bridge. Games can reacquaint you with the child in you who is anxious to come out and play.

Be Kind to Others

Doesn't it make you feel good to smile at another person or help someone in need? Most people would agree that being kind to others can improve your day, but it's now been shown that it can improve your health as well. Researchers at the Johns Hopkins Medical Institutions found that older adults who volunteer at troubled schools actually improve their own mental and physical health; this particular study showed a 50 percent decrease in cane usage by participants and a 44 percent increase in strength. Such activities allow older adults to remain active and engaged with others.

Helping others also fosters a personal sense of accomplishment, that in turn leads to lower rates of depression in individuals sixty-five and older (according to a recent compilation of research released by the Corporation for National and Community Service). Studies conducted with those who volunteered one hundred hours or more per year doing community service found a significant increase in health benefits, including fewer heart problems. Enhancing self-esteem can strengthen and enhance our immune systems by producing more T-cells, which help the body resist disease; endorphins are also released, and these stimulate the dilation of blood vessels and relax the heart. In fact, Harvard researchers found that just watching someone else perform an act of kindness can boost your immune system.

It doesn't take much to feel a warm glow in your chest and experience a newfound sense of energy after doing something nice for someone else. An extra smile for a cashier, a word of thanks to your mailman, an extra tip for the waitress—these are all small ways you can give to others and help yourself at the same time. You don't have to be a Peace Corps volunteer to benefit from the overall satisfaction of giving of yourself. The longevity benefits gained from doing something nice can be achieved simply by putting a few dollars in the Salvation Army kettle during the holidays or giving an extra donation at church.

It's also important to dream and then act on your dreams. Everything we see around us was the result of someone's dream, including the Post-it note or the cook's spatula. Inventors share the same characteristics: they act on their dreams; they are open-minded and willing to listen to others' suggestions; they are not afraid to fail—and if they do fail, they are willing to try again; they are aware of the things that they can change and those they can't. All these characteristics lead to a sense of balance and self-acceptance, which in turn leads to healthier and longer lives.

Our minds can be very negative and sometimes seem to be contrary to our own best interests. Our minds can make us think like spoiled children, go in wrong directions, and then—even worse—make us feel guilty. There are elusive reasons why our brains work that way, but on our journey to good health we want to change that way of thinking. We are going forward, in a positive direction, and we're adding miles to our journey with each small step. We are not in racecars competing with each other to win—instead, we are "braking" for health. We are allowing ourselves to savor each moment and reward ourselves whenever we can.

True enjoyment comes from activity of the mind and exercise of the body; the two are ever united.

—Karl Wilhelm von Humboldt

TEN STEPS I AM TAKING ON MY JOURNEY TO GOOD HEALTH

Liked the person I saw in the mirror

Took three deep breaths

Rented a comedy DVD

Learned a new word

Read the comics

Did a crossword puzzle

Listened to my favorite CD

Took a twenty-minute nap

Donated $10 to my favorite charity

Watched the sunset

Walking is the best possible exercise.

—Thomas Jefferson

CHAPTER EIGHT

PHYSICAL HEALTH

Stay Fit and Happy

Chapter 8: PHYSICAL HEALTH

It is commonly accepted that exercise—or activity, as I prefer to call it—is one of the best ways to improve your health and manage stress. Simply by adding a little movement to your life you can maintain flexibility, keep healthy bone mass, improve your mood, and ultimately even prevent heart disease. As Lynn Swann, former chair of the President's Council on Physical Fitness, emphasizes, "It's never too late to move for health." It has been shown that people who take up exercise at age seventy-five and quit smoking could add two years to their lives. It may take as little as thirty minutes a day, five days a weekto decrease your chances of heart disease, colon cancer, high blood pressure, or diabetes. However, if exercise is to become a part of your life, it should not be something you dread doing: adding activity to your lifestyle is not about drastic change, but rather about taking small steps to move your body in a way that is enjoyable to you. Most of all, avoid overly strenuous exercise—like walking too long or too far—to enhance your enjoyment. It really doesn't matter what kind of activity you engage in: The most important choice is whether you decide to be active at all. Experts agree that some activity, even a minimal amount, is better than none at all.

There are innumerable benefits, both physical and mental, to be gained from daily activity. Here is a list of some of them:

- » Lose weight

- » Reduce stress

- » Relieve depression and anxiety

- » Reduce risk of heart disease and certain cancers

- » Boost your mood

- » Give you more energy

- » Help you sleep better

- » Increase bone density

- » Strengthen your heart and lungs

- » Improve your quality of life

In fact, a good walk has been shown to be good for your head. According to Dr. Gary Small, professor of psychiatry and biobehavioral sciences at University of California, Los Angeles' (UCLA) Center on Aging, if the heart pumps more blood, it affects the brain because nutrients and oxygen-rich blood are being carried throughout the cells, thus improving brain function. Repetitive movement can actually stimulate certain areas of the brain, including the subcortical area, that is related to cognitive function—in other words, how well we think. Walking and talking is even better because the brain is engaging in a number of activities at the same time. In a 2008 issue of the *Harvard Health Letter*, it was reported that physical activity can both delay cognitive decline into dementia and even improve certain aspects of thinking.

It would take many pills to provide all of the benefits gained from physical activity. Activity is the one "pill" that can add years to your life, and it has no side effects. What's more, you can personalize your fitness program based on your own individual needs. Unlike pharmaceutical drugs that are prescribed to everyone alike, there is no one activity program that is prescribed for every body type.

According to the following guidelines suggested by the Mayo Clinic, before you start any activity program, be sure to check with your physician if:

» You're a man older than age forty or a woman older than age fifty
» You've had a heart attack
» You have a family history of heart disease before age fifty-five
» You have heart, lung, liver, or kidney disease
» You feel pain in your chest, joints, or muscles during physical activity
» You have high blood pressure, high cholesterol, diabetes, arthritis, osteoporosis, or asthma
» You've had joint replacement surgery
» You smoke
» You're overweight or obese
» You take medication to manage a chronic condition
» You have an untreated joint or muscle injury or persistent symptoms after a joint or muscle injury
» You're pregnant
» You're unsure of your health status

Even if you have a health condition such as arthritis, diabetes, or heart disease, it's important to be active: regular physical activity can improve your quality of life and reduce the risk of worsening your disease. A stronger heart, lungs, and muscles will allow you to go about your everyday tasks with greater ease. Exercise has also proven to be important in treating and preventing osteoporosis: even though bone mass peaks during the third decade of life, it has been shown that weight-bearing exercise such as walking, climbing stairs, and dancing can actually prevent its loss.

According to a 2008 report in *Circulation: Journal of the American Heart Association*, a study found that increased exercise levels are directly linked to a reduced risk of death. In this study—the largest known study to assess the link between fitness and mortality—15,660 men with various levels of fitness were tested. Highly fit men had half the risk of death compared to those with lowest levels of fitness. The risk of death was cut in half with an exercise program consisting of a brisk walk of about thirty minutes per day five to six times per week.

Once you start a physical activity program, remember to exercise in a safe manner and avoid injury. Try to choose activities that are appropriate for your fitness level. Build up the time you spend doing one activity before you switch to another that might take more effort. You also will want to invest in the proper equipment for the activity you choose—for example, a good pair of walking shoes—to maximize your effort. Invest in an inexpensive pair of dumbbells or a pair of stretchy tubes to help you strengthen your arms and upper back.

It's not surprising that people might resist taking part in an activity program: whereas eating is a necessity, staying active is clearly a matter of choice. However, given what we know about the value of exercise, it is rather shocking that a quarter of the American adult population still chooses not to participate in active pursuits. Given all the labor-saving devices available to us today, it's no wonder that our activity level has decreased over the past fifteen years. Even small things such as cell phones and remote controls for the TV have affected how much we move in our everyday lives.

Happily, we now have the freedom to choose what we want to do to get our bodies moving. The best news is that we can choose things that can even be fun. A healthy activity program can be incorporated into your daily schedule without meaning you must spend hours at the gym. If you're already planning a trip to the grocery store, park your car further away from the front door, or go to the mall and forego the escalator. At the supermarket, take extra time to walk down each aisle—every extra step is an extra moment of activity. Look for small ways to walk more: walk to the mailbox, take the dog for an extra walk, and get up to fetch your cell phone from the next room. Don't be a couch potato: use hand weights, ride a stationary bike, or simply do a few stretches as you watch your favorite TV show; try to avoid using the remote and get off the couch to change the channel or adjust the volume. Instead of sitting all day, try to find ways to stand, even if it means standing up while talking on the phone. Any activity counts!

Household chores don't have to be done vigorously to be a healthy form of activity. Doing the laundry or vacuuming the floor can allow you to both be productive and improve your health at the same time. Clean out that dresser that has been collecting junk, reorganize your bathroom cabinet, weed out old clothes from your closet, sweep out your garage: these activities will give you the pleasure of a job well done at the end of the day while at the same time allowing you to flex some muscle. Gardening is probably one of the best ways to add movement to your day while doing something rewarding—especially when neighbors admire your beautiful landscaping or you cut the colorful fresh flowers that result from your hard work. Outdoor work is the best way to burn calories while also strengthening your arms, legs, and back.

It's important to choose your activity wisely—whether it's swimming, playing golf, bike riding, or playing ping pong, find something that you really like to do. If you prefer group activities, find a walking group that does daily laps around a shopping mall, or start a lunchtime walking group with your co-workers. If you like to dance, check out the free dance lessons offered in some clubs and senior centers. You can also join a hiking group or golf league. Or you can simply make a date with a friend to go for a walk at a local park.

Sometimes simply getting started is the hardest part. There are many reasons keeping you from beginning a regular fitness program. Perhaps you haven't been active for a long time—in that case, you may want to choose something to start with that you enjoy doing, such as taking the dog for a short walk (the dog needs exercise just as you do). Another common excuse for not exercising is lack of time—but you can start with ten minutes of activity several days a week. Walk at work during a break or dance in the living room to your favorite music. You may feel that starting an activity program costs too much, but remember that you don't have to join a health club, invest in a stationary bike, or buy fancy exercise clothing. You can start simply by getting up thirty minutes earlier in the morning and doing some stretching.

Ten Ways to Get Going on an Activity Program

Start slowly. Even if it means walking from one room to the next, focus on increasing your movement a little each day until you get up to the maximum requirement set by the President's Council on Physical Fitness: thirty minutes of walking, five days a week.

» Listen to your body. If it hurts, stop; if it feels uncomfortable, slow down. You can do more harm by overdoing than by standing still.

» Stretch, stretch, stretch. Flexibility helps reduce injury, maintain balance, and can make activity easier all the way around.

» Drink water. It's important during any activity to stay hydrated; you will have more energy and will be less prone to suffering fatigue due to dehydration.

» Find a program or a friend. The best way to keep yourself on a program is to know that you have to meet someone who is waiting for you.

» Don't give up. Even if you skip a day or a week, be gentle on yourself and allow yourself a break. You can then restart with renewed energy and commitment.

» Remember that every activity counts, whether it's bathing the dog or picking fresh flowers.

» Take advice from professionals. As your activity program gets going, don't be afraid to take a lesson from a trainer or seek advice from others—it's a great way to rev up your motivation.

» Give yourself a reward at the end of the day. As you eat that small piece of dark chocolate, tell yourself that you worked hard to earn it.

» Enjoy what you do! Whether you resume the swimming sessions that you gave up as a child or just take a walk in the great outdoors, remember that activity does not have to be something you have to do, but something you enjoy doing.

There are basically two types of activity—aerobic and muscle strengthening—and each is equally important for your health: Aerobic, or "cardio," causes you to breathe harder and gets your heart beating faster. Activities such as brisk walking, riding a stationary bike, or pushing a lawn mower are activities that require moderate aerobic activity. Muscle-strengthening activities are recommended twice a week: these include lifting weights, working with resistance bands, practicing yoga, doing sit-ups or push-ups, or engaging in heavy gardening work.

Keeping track of what you do each week is a great way to monitor your activity progress. A workout record is the best thing you can do for yourself, and it doesn't matter if you use pen and paper, a workout book, or a spreadsheet. You can buy an exercise log in your local bookstore, or you can make one of your own following the examples below as suggested in the 2008 Physical Activity Guidelines for Americans published by the U.S. government (www.health.gov.).

"My doctor told me to start my exercise program very gradually. Today I drove past a store that sells sweat pants."

My aerobic activities this week

My goal is to do aerobic activities for a total of _____ hours and _____ minutes this week.

What I did	Effort	When I did it and for how long							Total hours or minutes
		Mon	Tue	Wed	Thu	Fri	Sat	Sun	
This is the total number of hours or minutes I did these activities this week:									

My strengthening activities this week

My goal is to do strengthening activities for a total of _____ days this week.

What I did	When I did it							Total days
	Mon	Tue	Wed	Thu	Fri	Sat	Sun	
This is the total number of days I did these activities this week:								

Here's a small warning about a voice you sometimes hear when you tell your body to exercise: it's your brain having a temper tantrum. Your mind can become willful and tempt you to do things that may not necessarily be good for you. Just like a spoiled child, it acts up at the worst times. You need to recognize that negative voice and laugh at it. So if you say, "I want to go for a walk," and your brain screams out, "Absolutely not," you can simply laugh. Sometimes a fierce internal battle may be in store, but it's up to you to face it and do what you know is good for you.

Most of all be sure to keep your activity simple. It is not necessary to completely change your life and try to head off in multiple directions all at once. Although you might get lost and go in the wrong direction every now and then, or even go backward, remember that you are on a scenic journey. The process is just as important as the destination, and every small step can be life altering.

Water Therapy

Lori Pullman, BPE, MA, wrote the water therapy section of this book. I met Lori at a Scripps Hospital Wellness retreat and was impressed with her presentation on water therapy. I followed her into the pool with several other health-minded individuals and I can assure you we all benefited from the experience. Lori's education and training are in sports science and kinesiology and with that training she is a master in the water. She resides in Canada and makes Calgary her home.

Lori believes that throughout the aging process, water is a life force; you were created from watery cells, you were born in a watery sac, and your body is 72 percent water. She explains that you can live without certain elements in nature, but water is not one of them. Water is used to revitalize the body's skin, circulatory system, muscles, and joints. It is essential for both internal use (daily intake to stay hydrated), as well as being used externally to soak, splash, steam, and sprinkle. Water is also beautiful and calming to look at and listen to in the form of waterfalls, rivers, and flowing streams. It is your companion for life, and it will improve your health in many ways.

There is a growing trend to use water as an environment for therapeutic forms of exercise that enhance mobility, increase range of motion, build strength, and develop stability for the aging body. These exercises—often referred to as hydrotherapy—have demonstrated a phenomenal record of improving health and wellness for those in their senior years. While your body may not be able to do certain things on land, it can certainly do them in an aquatic environment. Water exercise can be done as an individual program (see exercises below) or in a group.

Water makes perfect sense as a "total body" exercise regimen: every muscle of the body can be active in the water. First and foremost, the quality of buoyancy (ability to float) takes pressure off of joints, ligaments, and tendons. Secondly, the hydrostatic pressure of the water results in what we can refer to as a "massage effect" in which circulation, blood flow, and lymphatic function are enhanced. People often remark on how movement feels pain free in a pool, deep tank, jet tub, or soaker tub.

The larger joints of the shoulder and the hip support your body frame. These joints need to go through full ranges of motion every twenty-four hours or we lose flexibility in that area. Water exercise done daily (or at least three to four times per week) can help you regain back that mobility and provides the bonus of stronger muscles and improved levels of

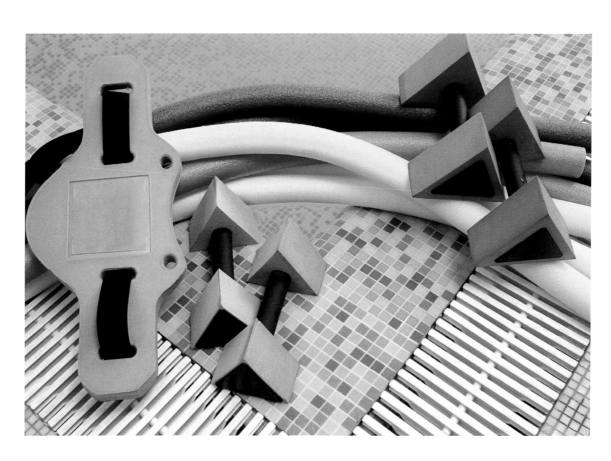

coordination. Water exercise is also a fantastic method for fall prevention, as you will find yourself to be more sure walking on land and are less likely to lose your balance.

The beauty of water therapy exercises is that each person can select a level of movement related to their current physical abilities. You do not have to be part dolphin to use the water environment—in fact; most exercises can be accomplished in waist-high water along the side of a pool. First, seek out a local swimming pool or spa in your area that is close and convenient. The pool should have safety features that will make it a suitable place to exercise: You should consider the pool's temperature (moving in warmer water is more enjoyable and may aid in ease of movement), cleanliness, the chemicals in the water, availability of ramps and rails (many pool facilities provide access to the water even from a wheelchair), and ease of access to locker rooms/bathrooms. It is a good idea, of course, to always have another person with you in a water environment (pool, lake, spa); the buddy system is not only safer, but it enhances the enjoyment of water exercise. If you're interested in taking a class, be sure to ask about whether the instructors have certification in therapeutic water exercise.

Because water exercise brings quick results, you may discover the benefits of "playing in the water" within just a few short weeks. Each exercise—often performed to music to enhance the movement's rhythm and flow—may be repeated between fifty and one hundred times: this is possible because water allows for high-volume repetitions due to the reduced stress on joints. People adopting this form of exercise begin to feel younger and more mobile and report a reduction in body pain and joint stiffness.

Please see your physician before beginning any exercise program. Now, come along and let's move in the water!

Exercise 1: *Walking in the Water*

Body Position/Description: Begin walking in the shallow water, back and forth at various speeds, from long strides to a trot or jog.

Equipment: Optional use of a flotation device such as a water noodle/tube or flutterboard.

Position of Equipment: Hold the flotation device with both hands in front of the body.

Stance: Keep your feet moving with your heels pressing down to the pool floor; avoid walking on the toes.

Variation: Your water-walking warm-up can be varied from forward movements to backward walking to a sideways walk; mix it up a bit as you become accustomed to the water temperature.

Exercise 2: *The Water Bicycle*

Body Position/Description: Holding a flotation device (water noodle or flutterboard), lean your body back slightly so that your feet are off the pool bottom, or try deeper water if you are a good swimmer. Pretend you are sitting on a bicycle and begin to pedal, with your knees flexing and extending.

Equipment: Water noodle or flutterboard.

Position of Equipment: Hold the water noodle under your armpits and lean back.

Stance: Feet are off the bottom of the pool at all times.

Variation: When you master the bicycle motion, move the body in a 360-degree turn to the right or left by staying upright. You will have to tread in a sideways bicycle motion to complete the full circle.

Exercise 3: Water Sit-up

Body Position/Description: Lean back and float. Bend both knees at the same time into the chest with your toes flexed towards your shins. Follow this with a full extension of the knees. Tighten the abdominal muscles as you complete this modified sit-up in the water.

Equipment: Water noodle works best.

Position of Equipment: Hold water noodle under your armpits as it wraps around your back.

Stance: Feet are off the pool floor; tip slightly backward to raise both knees at the same time to the chest and straighten the legs out again. Repeat until you feel fatigued.

Exercise 4: Pool-Side Leg Lift

Body Position/Description: With the left or right side of your body facing the pool wall, lift the outside leg laterally (sideways) while standing on the support leg. Raise and lower the leg with a powerful movement. Swing it as high as is comfortable, then force the limb back down through the water with equal pressure or thrust.

Equipment: No equipment required.

Stance: Feet are on the bottom of the pool, slightly more than shoulder–width apart, heels flat. Hip is sideways to the wall. Raise the leg with force.

Exercise 5: Upright Hamstring Curl

Body Position/Description: Holding on to the pool edge/wall, stand in waist- or hip-deep water. Kick one heel up towards the buttocks, squeezing the muscles tightly until the heel almost touches your bottom.

Equipment: No equipment required.

Stance: Feet shoulder-width apart; the exercising leg lifts to the rear/posterior.

Variation: Alternate legs, switching from left to right at a quicker pace as you kick your heels to your bottom.

Exercise 6: Deep Water Strides

Body Position/Description: In deeper water, begin to stride with your legs as if you were cross-country skiing. The movement is generated by the hip, and the knees are straight as you stride forward.

Equipment: Flutterboard is useful.

Position of Equipment: Hold hands on the sides of the board, which is held out in front of the body.

Stance: Long lateral strides as if taking big steps. As your legs move in deeper water, do not let feet touch the bottom of the pool.

Exercise 7: Water Torso Twist

Body Position/Description: Standing in chest-high water, twist the body side-to-side. Create force by pushing the water as you gently rotate in a twisting motion. This demonstrates torque through your torso/upper body.

Equipment: Water noodle.

Position of Equipment: Hold water noodle with a shoulder-width grip in front of the body.

Stance: The feet are placed in a wide star shape/straddle on the bottom of the pool with the heels flat.

Variation: As you warm up, see if you can slowly increase the range of the twisting motion by lifting one heel at a time; this will cause the body to turn more. This exercise is great for enhancing a golf swing or tennis stroke.

Exercise 8: Water Chest Press

Body Position/Description: Push the water noodle/tube off the chest and back to the body in a smooth repetitive movement. The water tube should push as much water away as you draw back in for the movement. Keep your shoulders slightly under the water level.

Equipment: Water noodle/tube.

Position of Equipment: Grip water noodle/tube at slightly more than shoulder width with a wide grip.

Stance: Feet are flat on the pool floor with heels down and knees slightly bent.

Exercise 9: Water Star-Lateral Straddle

Body Position/Description: Float on your back. From your hips, create a wide lateral movement with both legs—in other words, a horizontal star shape. Force water in and away by squeezing the legs in and out while keeping the knees straight.

Equipment: Water noodle

Position of Equipment: Wrap the noodle around your waist.

Stance: Floating on your back with head slightly upright.

Exercise 10: Meditation Float

Body Position/Description: Free float in a comfortable position on your back. Float with no kicking—allow the water to support you. Take deep breaths through the nose and blow out gently through your mouth. Think calm and positive thoughts. Imagine a pain-free body and smile!

Equipment: Two water noodles/tubes.

Position of Equipment: One noodle placed at back of neck; one noodle on the waist behind the low back.

Stance: Free floating in a large, open water space.

Gentle Yoga

I recently attended a medical conference sponsored by Cleveland Clinic. (If you live near one of their facilities, you are very fortunate. This hospital is on the cutting edge of medical care and practices integrative medicine on all levels.) The conference started at 6:30 each morning, which is earlier than I would normally get going. At that first session, the moderator asked a room of about four hundred physicians and scientists to stand up and do yoga, and the murmur from the audience was immediately audible: He is kidding, right? As we all dutifully stood, we did not know what to expect. It turned out that the yoga program was very easy to do, even for those of us who had to use a chair to steady ourselves.

If you are like me, when you hear the word "yoga" you immediately wonder: Will I have to be flexible, or do I have to stand on my head or touch my toes? There is a little voice in my head saying, I have a bad knee; I have a weight problem; I can't do those poses; I have a bad back, so how can I twist into those positions? There are many styles and variations of yoga, just as there are many styles and forms of exercise. Our reason for introducing you to yoga in this book is to show you how accessible, easy, enjoyable, health giving, and rewarding gentle yoga can be for you.

Judi Bar works with the Cleveland Clinic and specializes in treating chronic pain, and through her practice she has heard it all. She says there are many misconceptions about yoga that keep people from trying it for the first time. The truth is that yoga has only one requirement: You have to know how to breathe. By practicing yoga you gain flexibility over time, and eventually you can even touch your toes. And there are headstands in yoga, but only for advanced students. Different postures can be adapted to accommodate physical limitations or injuries. Physical challenges, age, or body type should not keep you from trying yoga. In fact, even people who are bedridden or in wheelchairs should be practicing yoga. Judi teaches five to six group classes a day and sees several students privately; she also teaches yoga workshops, yoga teacher classes, and yoga therapy certification classes. The yoga she teaches is derived from traditional yoga postures.

Postures are broken down to isolate certain muscle groups and body systems. In addition to the obvious benefits gained from moving your body, including lubricating your joints and stretching and strengthening your muscles, yoga can stimulate the blood flow to your other body systems to prevent or treat different disease processes and calm the nervous system. By promoting a deep awareness of your breath and exerting a calming effect on your body, yoga can help you feel relaxed yet energized. We are the ultimate recyclers of energy: as we learn to relax tight muscles with our breath awareness, tension is released and is converted into vital energy for us.

The benefits of yoga are numerous and are still being discovered. With regular practice, you will see the difference in your life. Some of the things yoga can do for you are:

- » Support bone strength for osteoporosis sufferers
- » Increase range of motion and lessen pain in all of the joints, including for those individuals with such conditions as osteoarthritis, tendonitis, and bursitis
- » Gain better muscle strength and resiliency
- » Improve balance for better coordination
- » Support healthy feet, knees, spine, hips, and shoulders
- » Support the immune system
- » Improve respiration, circulation, and digestion
- » Reduce stress by calming the central nervous system
- » Add to better memory recall and concentration
- » Develop higher-quality sleep
- » Increase confidence and a better outlook on life
  (a "go-with-the-flow" type of feeling)

Yoga can work for you whether you are in chronic pain or you just want to feel better. Judi Bar developed the following program, and we hope you give it a try. Please see your physician before beginning any exercise program.

Gentle Yoga Sequence

Simple items that will be needed for this yoga program are:

> A firm chair with a back
>
> A yoga strap (a robe tie or dog leash can work)
>
> No shoes, comfortable clothing
>
> A relaxation CD playing in a quiet room

We would like to remind you to remember to sit and stand straight even when you are not practicing yoga—this opens up your lungs for better breathing, strengthens your core muscles, and aids in better digestion. Remind yourself to breathe when you find yourself in sticky situations, which will help you to be more mindful in your choices.

Also, only go to your edge of stretching—you should not feel a fiery, knife-edged feeling, but rather as if you are reaching into the tightness. We don't push through pain; we listen to our bodies and move to our edge, gently breathe, and then release. If your body tells you that it is doing something it should not do, then listen. What distinguishes yoga from other exercises is breath awareness and mindfulness.

You don't have to do all of the postures in this routine all at once. Perhaps choose several postures to do in the morning, some to do during the day, and finish with a few in the evening. These postures can complement any lifestyle. Remember, we are more prone to injuries over time if we don't stretch and counteract continual muscle movement.

Seated Breathing

Begin sitting with your back straight and tall, away from the back of the chair; feet are planted firmly on the floor, knees straight ahead of you, hands resting in your lap. This will be your position while doing postures on the chair. Relax your eyes, jaw, shoulders, and belly. Take several deep breaths and notice what it feels like. Now release your belly and take a deep breath, allowing your belly to expand (put your hands on your belly) when you breathe in and contract when you exhale. Take five deep belly breaths this way, and then see how you feel.

Neck Rolls

Keep your neck tall, and with shoulders dropped, lower your chin to your chest. Gently roll your right ear to the right shoulder; gently roll slightly back (not too far). Roll your left ear to your left shoulder, and then return chin to chest. Do this two times slowly while keeping the belly breathing, and then reverse the movement and circle to the left. Notice how you feel and note whether or not you can keep the breathing going as you move.

Note: The breathing is important for circulation and will also help to calm your mind; the rolls loosen up your neck, which helps to prevent headaches.

Fan Pose

Sit further forward on the front of your chair with a straight spine. Reach your arms behind you and grab the chair at the highest point you can reach without feeling pain. Pull your shoulder blades back and lean forward, leading with your heart center and chin. Take three deep breaths and feel your heart center opening.

Note: This stretches your rotator cuffs, brings more circulation to your upper front body, and expands your lung capacity.

Seated Cat Pose

Remain sitting forward on the chair, inhale, and push your spine forward, gently looking up. Now exhale and curl your spine down, feeling as if you are reaching your mid-back towards the chair back. Do this three times.

Note: Articulating the spine brings more blood to the area, softens the muscles, and activates the nervous system.

Sun Breath

Press your buttocks into the chair, open your legs as wide as you can, make sure there is no pain and leave enough room for you to drop your head down, drop your arms to your sides, then scoop them from your sides towards the ceiling with an inhale while gently looking up, then exhale and roll your spine down as far as you can. Open your legs enough that you can drop your head down (if you have blood pressure problems, glaucoma, or gastroesophogeal reflux disease (GERD), don't drop your head down as far). Do these three times; the last time you dip your head towards the ground, remain in that position for one breath.

Note: This posture increases range of motion for the shoulders, allows for deeper spinal articulation, and stimulates the lymph system to pump.

Groin Stretch

Open legs as wide as possible while still keeping your back straight (this keeps the connective tissue activated) and place your hands on your knees. Inhale and gently move forward slightly to stretch your groin; on the exhale; come back to a straight seated position. Do this three times, and then hold the forward position for one breath.

Note: This works the pelvic floor, supporting your bladder, increasing blood flow to the male and female organs, and stretching the groin muscles that, when tight, can cause knee and lower back problems.

Arms and Shoulders

Keep your legs wide, arms straight out to the side; shoulder blades are pulled back and palms are turned to the sides and up. Inhale and hold the inhale for a moment, and then exhale with a sigh. Do this three times.

Note: This strengthens your shoulders and expands your lung capacity. Be aware of how you feel when your let your arms drop to your sides—this way you can better recognize tension in your body and relax.

Wide-legged Lower Back Twist

Continuing to keep the legs wide, gently push your right hand into the inside of your right knee, then rotate your right shoulder forward by pushing on your right hand. Begin to twist and look to your left, keeping your buttocks on the chair. Stay in the twist for three breaths; on the exhale, come back to neutral. Reverse the position and take your time feeling the lower back stretch. Repeat on the left side.

Note: Try to feel a stretch in your lower sacrum area (the large triangular bone at the base of the spine; we are increasing blood flow to that area.

Seated Spinal Twist

Stay sitting forward on the chair. Keep your spine long and buttocks pressed into the seat; knees are together. Lengthen your spine as you inhale, then place your right hand on the outside of your left knee and place your left hand low on the back of the chair, keeping your shoulders even and parallel to the ground. Look over your left shoulder. Don't force the twist or cause pain in your back. Perform an even, long stretch: inhale while lengthening your spine, and on the exhale twist just a bit further. Hold for three breaths.

Note: This posture softens your spine, wrings out tension in your spine, and squeezes the organs and glands on the side you are twisting, then soaks the same organs and glands when you release the twist.

Leg Stretch

Sit straight, left leg directly in front of your left hip. Cross your right leg over your left leg, placing your right ankle near your left knee (see below if you are not able to cross your leg over your thigh). Notice that if you round your back, you lose the stretch. Gently pulse the crossed leg in this position—this will begin to loosen your hip flexors—as you continue to breathe in and out. Then stop the motion, place your hands on your knee and ankle, and gently lean forward (leading with your heart center and chin, keeping your spine long) with a breath. Do this for five breaths, being sure to keep your back straight. Release and do the other side. For a variation, straighten your left leg to lessen the stress on your right knee, and use a strap to hold the leg there. Try to get the knee bent as much as possible to stretch deeper into the hip.

Note: This is a very important stretch to prevent or treat certain types of sciatica as it stretches the piriformis (a muscle in the buttocks), which is never naturally stretched.

Hip Circles

Stand up straight; keep your knees loose, and your toes moving. Use a chair for balance if you wish (you don't want to tweak your knees by planting your feet down). Keep your buttocks tucked and do a figure-eight with your hips, and then hip circles.

Note: These movements lubricate your hip joints.

Gene Kelly Stretch

Standing on your left foot, cross your right foot over your left (hold onto a chair if you wish). Now push your right hip out to the right and bring your right arm up to bend to the left. Hold for three breaths.

Note: This stretches the side of your hip and works the upper and front parts of your hip. It can ease bursitis by stretching the iliotibial band, which is always tight in most people.

Mountain Pose with Feet Together

Stand straight, top of head lifting toward the ceiling, shoulders pulled back and down. Your belly is pulled in, tailbone tucked, knee bones lifting upward, and feet flat. Place your hands in the prayer position in front of you, at your heart center. Stand still and take three deep breaths. Close your eyes and take an additional three breaths. Notice what it feels like to balance with your eyes closed. Staying in mountain pose, slowly rise up on your tiptoes on the inhale, slowly lower down on your exhale. Do this three times. Use the chair to help you balance.

Note: This is beneficial for stamina, balance, and patience; it also strengthens your feet and ankles and supports the proprioceptive response.

Symmetrical Stretch

Stand on your tiptoes and raise your arms to the ceiling. Keeping your navel pulled toward your spine for stability, lower down, keeping your arms in the air as you press your heels into the ground. On an inhale, continue to reach up, and on the exhale concentrate on pressing your heels to the ground. Feel the energy pass through your spine as you work to lengthen your spine.

Note: This posture minutely extends the distance between the vertebrae, increasing blood flow and hydration to the spine; it also helps maintain your height and counters gravity.

Deep Knee Bends and Spinal Stabilization

Stand close to your chair for balance in order to take pressure off your back. Place your feet about three inches apart and keep your toes pointing forward. Bend your knees as you press your heels into the floor and keep your buttocks tucked. Breathe; stay in this position for at least three breaths. If your knees and quadriceps (front thigh muscles) are weak, stand with your back against a wall and do posture there. Lean forward just slightly. If your back feels weak or sore, place your arms on your legs or on a chair.

Note: This posture strengthens your quadriceps and groin, which will support strong knees and back. When you lean slightly forward, you are doing a spinal stabilization of your lower back.

Tree Pose

Stand on your right foot and gently place your left foot at your ankle, with toes touching the ground. Use a chair for support if you feel unstable. Stand straight and pull your navel in towards your spine. After you become comfortable with this position, you can begin to lift the left foot off the ground and higher up on your leg. Also you can put your hands in the Namaste position or prayer pose to take the pose a bit deeper. Hold for at least five breaths. Repeat, standing on your left foot and raising your right foot/leg.

Note: This posture helps maintain your strength while increasing patience and body awareness.

Warrior I

Place a chair in front of you with the side of the chair on your left. With both of your feet pointing directly forward, place your right foot on the seat of the chair and press your left heel into the ground. Lengthen your spine and begin to move your body forward (put your hand on your hip to make it a bit harder if your wish), breathe, and begin to do a slight backbend; continue to breathe. Hold this for at least three breaths. Pull your body back and straighten your right leg on the chair to stretch the back of your right leg. Hold for at least three breaths. Reverse and repeat on the other side.

Note: This posture helps stretch your Achilles tendons and calf muscles that, if tight, can cause heel spurs and plantar fasciitis (a painful foot condition). As you push forward and lean back, your psoas (which helps to rotate the hip joint and flex the spine) is being stretched; if the psoas is tight or unbalanced, it can pull on your lower back and knee.

Quad Stretch

Stand facing the chair, keeping both feet pointed forward, hands on your hips, put your right foot on the seat of the chair; flex the foot so that the bottom of your foot faces the ceiling. Now bend your supporting leg to stretch your quadriceps muscles (the large muscles on the front of the thigh). If you don't feel much of a stretch, sit down and hold onto the seat back, grab your ankle with your hand or your strap, and keep your knees together. Allow yourself to hold this position for at least three breaths.

Note: This stretches the quadriceps, which, when tight, can pull on your knees and lower back.

Shoulder Loops

Stand with your feet hip distance apart and hold the strap loosely in front of you in both hands. On an inhale, bring the strap over your head to a taut position and on an exhale, lower the strap behind you as low as you can, keeping the strap symmetrical (in other words, don't let one arm loop over without the other). Do this at least three times.

Note: This movement gives your shoulders a good range of motion and warms the synovial fluid in your shoulders.

Tighten the strap several notches keep it taut and loop it over your head to a tight spot, using your breath to lengthen and expand the width of your stretch.

Note: This further opens up your shoulders, stimulates the immune system, and opens up your lungs, enabling deeper breathing.

Ninety-degree Stretch

Stand with the chair in front of you with the back of it facing you. Hold onto the top back of the chair and walk backwards, bending forward with your arms. The closer your feet are, the tighter the stretch for the back of your legs and your lower back. Don't put too much weight on your arms as this can hurt your shoulders. Hold for at least three deep breaths. Look up slightly and take two breaths, then move your head back between your arms and wag your tail to massage the small muscles in your back.

Note: These movements are wonderful stretches for your entire back as they lengthen the spine and stretch your shoulders; they also provide a stretch for your hamstrings, those large and often tight muscles at the back of our thighs.

Stand in Mountain Pose

Place your hands behind you at your waist, or if your neck is sensitive, place them behind your head, tuck your chin, inhale as you lengthen your spine and begin to look up. Do a gentle back bend, and continue to breathe.

Note: This posture helps alleviate depression as we open the heart, increasing blood flow to the upper front of the body.

Lion Pose

Standing up straight, inhale and then exhale. Open your eyes wide, stick your tongue out by opening your mouth wide, and say "ahhhhhh." Do this three times.

Note: Because this pose opens your jaw and increases blood flow to the area, it is helpful for those with temporomandibular joint disorder (TMJ, a painful jaw disorder); it also sends blood flowing to your throat area (By the way, kids love this pose also!).

Relaxation

Either sit on a chair or lie down on a bed or sofa, or lie down on the floor. Find something to place over your eyes if you are lying down. Now begin to slow your breath down. Listen to the sounds in the room and breathe gently as you relax each part of your body, letting all of your body systems catch up. Breathe gently and easily for three or four minutes. Stretch your arms upward, and then bring your hands down to your heart center in the prayer position. Think of something that you are grateful for today and gently move through your day with awareness and ease. Repeat this exercise several times until fully relaxed.

Always check with your physician before starting any new exercise program. If you have injuries or a physical problem, you might want to work with a yoga therapist; these therapists are trained to help you work with physical challenges. If you want to take your yoga practice even further and are interested in taking a class, look for one labeled "gentle," "restorative," "chair," or "therapeutic." It is important to confirm that the teacher is registered as a certified teacher with Yoga Alliance. A list of teachers in your area can be found at the Web sites of the following organizations: International Association of Yoga Therapists (www.iayt.org), Yoga Journal (www.yogajournal.com), and Yoga Alliance (www.yogaalliance.org).

Spoil Yourself with a Massage

In this fast-paced world, massage can do more than provide physical relief: It's a sure-fire way to decrease anxiety, enhance sleep quality, improve your concentration, and give you greater energy. After a massage, many people report feeling a sense of perspective and clarity. The capacity of touch to invoke a sense of stillness and calm is perhaps one reason why massage can be so effective in treating stress. Massage also unlocks physical tension in the body, thus easing pain in stiff or injured muscles, and it acts as a boost to the circulatory system. Breathing may deepen as you become more relaxed through massage.

Massage is an indulgence that can add years to your life—it may add to your weekly expenses, but it is worth the cost. If you don't want to spend the money for a full massage, you can also try self-massage in places that are easy to reach, such as your arms, hands, and feet, or ask a friend or partner to apply pressure firm enough to indent the skin to places in the body that are tender or sore (or even places that are not necessarily where it hurts). You'll be surprised at how good it can feel.

A form of therapy that dates back to ancient times, massage today is practiced in many different forms using various techniques. In order to help you decide which type of massage you would like to receive, the most popular forms are described below; Associated Bodywork and Massage Professionals provided these descriptions.

Swedish Massage

This is the most common type of massage therapy in the United States. Massage therapists use long smooth strokes, kneading, and circular movements on superficial layers of muscle using massage lotion or oil. Swedish massage therapy can be very gentle and relaxing. If you've never had massage before, this is a good one to try first.

Aromatherapy Massage

Aromatherapy massage is traditional Swedish massage with the addition of one or more scented plant oils to address specific needs. The massage therapist can select oils that are relaxing, energizing, stress-reducing, balancing, etc. (one of the most common essential oils used in aromatherapy massage is lavender, which is calming). Aromatherapy massage is particularly suited to stress-related conditions or conditions with an emotional component.

Hot Stone Massage

Smooth heated stones are placed on certain points on the body to warm and loosen tight muscles and balance energy centers. The massage therapist may also hold stones and apply gentle pressure with them. Hot stone massage is good for people who have muscle tension but prefer lighter massage.

Deep Tissue Massage

Deep tissue massage targets the deeper layers of muscle and connective tissue. The massage therapist uses slower strokes or friction techniques across the grain of the muscle. Deep tissue massage is used for chronically tight or painful muscles, repetitive strain, postural problems, or recovery from injury. People often feel sore for one to two days after deep tissue massage.

Shiatsu

Shiatsu is a form of Japanese bodywork that uses localized finger pressure in a rhythmic sequence on acupuncture meridians. Each point is held for two to eight seconds to improve the flow of energy and help the body regain balance.

Thai Massage

Like shiatsu, Thai massage aligns the energies of the body using gentle pressure on specific points. Thai massage also includes compressions and stretches. You don't just lie there: instead, the therapist moves and stretches you into a sequence of postures—it's like yoga without you having to do any work. Thai massage is more energizing than other forms of massage; it also reduces stress and improves flexibility and range of motion.

Pregnancy Massage

Also called prenatal massage, pregnancy massage is becoming increasingly popular with expectant mothers. Massage therapists who are certified in this type of massage know the proper way to position and support the woman's body during the session as well as how to modify techniques.

Reflexology

Although reflexology is sometimes called foot massage, it is more than simply massage done on the feet. Reflexology involves applying pressure to certain points on the foot that correspond to organs and systems in the body. Reflexology is very relaxing, especially for people who stand all day or just have tired, achy feet.

Sports Massage

Sports massage is specifically designed for people who are involved in physical activity. However, you don't have to be a professional athlete to have one: it's also enjoyed by people who are active and work out often. The focus in sports massage isn't on relaxation but rather on preventing and treating injury and enhancing athletic performance.

If you prefer not to spend money on a professional massage, there are basic massage techniques that you can practice at home, either on yourself or on a partner. There are also many massage devices—both manual and electric—on the market that may aid in self-massage. Here are a few strokes you can practice to hone your own massage technique:

Fan Stroking

Place your hands side by side on the body, palms down, and then smoothly and gently slide upward, leading with your fingers. Use the weight of your body to apply a steady, even pressure. Fan your hands out to both sides of the body and slide them down the sides, molding them to the contours of the body. Repeat.

Circular Stroking

Place your hands pointing away from you on one side of the body. Circle your hands in a clockwise direction, one hand at a time. As one arm meets the other, lift your hand over, rejoining the body on the other side to finish the circle. Repeat.

Thumb Stroking

Follow steps for circular stroking using your thumbs. Stroke firmly upward and out to the side with the left thumb and follow with the right thumb, building up a steady rhythm. Repeat.

Basic Kneading

This movement is much like kneading dough and is useful on the fleshy areas of the body, such as the hips. Place your hands flat on the body with elbows apart and fingers pointing away from you. With your right hand, gently grasp some flesh and release it into your left hand. Repeat with the left hand. Keep your strokes rhythmic.

Recent studies show that regular massage provides surprising health benefits in the treatment of hypertension, arthritis, burns, and simple surgery. Above and beyond specific physical benefits, relaxing with a massage is another wonderful way to slow down, treasure the moment, and enjoy the journey.

When it comes to any kind of physical activity, whether it means doing the dishes, walking the dog, or relaxing your muscles with a massage, doing something is better than nothing, and even a small amount of movement is better than none. If you find something that makes you happy and gets you moving, then you have gone a thousand miles on your journey to good health. Keep a journal and watch how quickly all the little things you do accumulate. You'll be amazed at how far you can go!

TEN STEPS I AM TAKING ON MY JOURNEY TO GOOD HEALTH

Woke up and stretched my arms over my head

Walked to the mailbox

Put away my TV remote and read instead

Got up thirty minutes earlier

Began an Activity Journal

Walked up and down four flights of stairs

Walked at the mall for an hour

Planted some flower bulbs in the yard

Asked a friend to meet me for a coffee and a walk

Gave myself a leg massage

The only limit to our realization of tomorrow will be our doubts of today.

—Franklin D. Roosevelt

CHAPTER NINE

THE FUTURE IS NOW

Get Ready for the Wonders of Technology

Chapter 9: THE FUTURE IS NOW

If you have made it this far in your journey to longevity and health, your future looks bright. Nanotechnology and biotechnology are advancing faster than you are aging. For every year you age, biotechnology is gaining on you by about five to ten years. It is an extraordinary time in the field of science, and you are the beneficiary.

Every additional year you live, science is discovering genetic codes that, when switched on or off, have the potential to treat or cure diseases, reverse aging, and repair damaged organs. Within a decade there is the chance that those confined to wheelchairs will be walking, and those who have lost their sight will see. These scientific advancements have a direct impact on your life span. In fact, one extremely confident biomedical gerontologist from Cambridge University believes the first person to live to one thousand has already been born, and that advances made in stem cell research, gene therapy, and other new techniques can stop the aging process altogether!

It is easy to get caught up in the news of the day, which is often filled with negative images of war and violence. What we are not exposed to on a daily basis is the good news, and there is a lot more of that than the bad. If you could just take a one-week break from watching or reading the news and instead go the library or bookstore and pick up a book on the future of health care (health care without pharmaceutical companies), you will start healing within your own mind and body. This could add seven years to your life. And making it through one extra decade of your life could actually add two additional decades.

The shift away from the troubling era of big pharmaceutical companies cannot come quickly enough for many of us in the sixty-plus crowd. Within just a few years we will look back on the drugs we put into our bodies and wonder what we were thinking. Chemotherapy, today's wonder treatment, will most likely become an oddity of medicine in a few short years. Treating conditions with drugs alone is a deadly form of medicine—it does not take into consideration those deaths that are preventable in a wellness health care system that deals with diseases before they become life threatening. To give you an example of how far we have come, at the turn of the twentieth century, thousands of people flocked to spas and health centers to dip into water that was radioactive, because they had been led to believe that radioactive materials were the new "wonder cure" for everything. Marie Curie and her husband Pierre made many important discoveries about radioactive materials, but Marie and Pierre paid a high price, dying from its poisonous effects. We are headed toward an entirely new approach to our health: It will be "health care," not "disease care." The focus will be on prevention, that in the past has only included such things as cancer screenings and blood pressure checks, often done well after the early onset of disease was detected. In the future, we will use diagnostic testing to determine what genetic potentials we have, good and bad. We will devise a plan that will allow us to take control of our medical destinies and live to be well over 120 and still enjoy excellent health.

Some of this diagnostic testing is available to you right now. As noted in Chapter Two, genetic testing can be done for less than $500; while today's tests won't give you the detailed information that future genetic testing will provide, it may help you alter your course and add years to your life. One diagnostic test that we all have done routinely has so much to offer; however, bear in mind that when we get a blood test, most of us fail to have our nutrient levels checked. Simply knowing what nutrients are depleted in your body and then making positive changes could add ten to fifteen years to your life.

While there are fantastic advances being made every day in the fields of biotechnology and nanotechnology, we still have to make one old-fashioned choice that is fundamental to our survival: We have to commit to a healthy lifestyle and make some positive changes. Science cannot save us from ourselves. We must take responsibility for what we put into our bodies, so it is up to us to stop taking prescription drugs whose side effects are killing hundreds of thousands of us each year. We can also toss out the government's food pyramid in favor of one that makes a lot of sense. All we have to do is stop and think about it.

- GFR (NON-AFRICAN AMER.)
- GFR (AFRICAN AMER.)
- SODIUM
- POTASSIUM
- CHLORIDE
- BICARBONATE
- CALCIUM
- BILIRUBIN, TOT
- TOTAL PROTEIN
- ALBUMIN
- AST (SGOT)
- ALT (SGPT)
- AL...

	Range
88	65-110 (mg/dl
8	8-18 (mg/dL)
0.7	0.5-1.5 (mg/d
>60	- (mL/min)
>60	- (mL/min)
142	135-145 (mE
3.7	3.5-5.0 (mEq
98	97-107 (mE
29	24-31 (mEq
9.4	8.8-10.3 (m
0.9	<1...
7.1	

Make Way for Biotechnology

Biotechnology involves the use of biological systems and living organisms to create or modify products and processes involved in agriculture, medicine, or food science. It combines such disciplines as genetics, microbiology, biochemistry, and robotics, among other things. Sometimes referred to today as "genetic engineering," biotechnology encompasses many more procedures for modifying organisms for the needs of humanity. This wide-ranging discipline has resulted in amazing results, as shown in the following examples:

Growing New Blood Vessels and Using Simple Injection to Avoid Surgery

Today thousands of patients undergo risky surgery to repair damaged heart tissue and diseased blood vessels. While millions of lives have been saved with these procedures and the benefits are undeniable, within a decade this type of surgery could be replaced by a simple procedure involving so-called progenitor cells. Research being done in Germany, at Harvard Medical School, and Children's Hospital Boston demonstrates that progenitor cells easily obtained from a patient's blood or bone marrow can grow to become various sorts of adult cells. The progenitor cells used in the Harvard study grew into full-fledged blood vessel systems in the laboratory mice. The work being done at Harvard could eventually be used to treat a number of conditions where new blood vessels would be vital to recovery, such as treatment of severe wounds and cardiovascular disease.

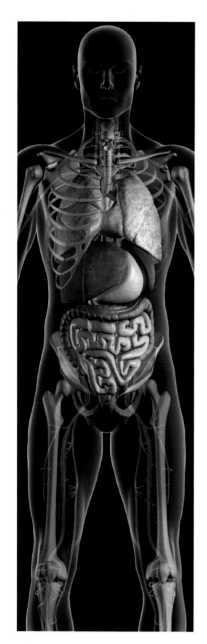

Growing New Organs – Regenerative Medicine

The field of regenerative medicine has already arrived. Scientists, working with highly specialized surgeons, are using extracellular matrix material (the material that surrounds every cell in our bodies and allows them to survive) and the patient's own cells to grow new bladders, blood vessels, heart valves, fingers and more. We are already taking patients off transplant lists and growing organs from their own cells within weeks. How this works is; some of a patient's own cells are harvested and taken to a specialized laboratory where the cells are incorporated into a cellular matrix material. The material serves as a platform for tissue regeneration and differentiation. Our cells are constantly regenerating through special signaling processes orchestrated by our DNA, now we are doing it when the body fails in its repair process. This is not some theory that presents as tomorrow's promise; this is medicine being practiced today and we can all look forward to its continued life-and-limb saving advancement. Follow this technology closely because it may save your life someday, and that time is soon.

It's Good to Be Cool

The future of medicine is "cool" in more ways than you can imagine. At The University of Iowa, scientists are working to understand the biological processes of hibernating animals. Research has shown that these animals have a morphine-like substance in their blood, and scientists are looking at ways to re-create the hibernating effect in humans through the use of a simple injection. In the future we may be able to keep people alive in a hibernating state for up to a few months; this may buy them enough time to get a much-needed organ transplant or just enough time to keep them alive as they are being transported from a serious car accident to the emergency room. In a world where seconds and minutes can save lives, think about the benefits of gaining several months.

Surgeons already place patients undergoing cardiovascular surgery into a hypothermic state by reducing their body temperature to 85 degrees prior to surgery, because the body slows down at lowered temperatures and survival rates are improved. Within a few years we will know a lot more about how "being cool" will save lives. Seemingly simple technologies and concepts can actually offer big lifesaving benefits.

The Wonders of Genetic Testing

By far the most exciting breakthroughs in the fields of geriatrics and longevity are being made through genetic testing. With more and more people living into their hundreds, scientists are now able to identify and isolate genes that may be protecting centenarians today—and all of us in the future—from age-related diseases that have not only shortened our lives but have detrimentally affected our healthy lifestyles. For example, genetic factors can contribute to 57 percent of the risk for heart attack in men; other genetic mutations currently being identified are those that are markers for multiple sclerosis, diabetes, and lupus.

New genes are constantly being discovered, and the field of gene testing is evolving before our eyes. A discipline that was virtually nonexistent twenty years ago, gene testing has made tremendous strides and is destined to uncover more specific, critical information linking genes to disease. If you are at a high risk for certain diseases based on family history, your future and that of your children may be determined through genetic testing.

Types of Genetic Testing

Diagnostic: Identifies or rules out a specific genetic or chromosomal condition and is used to confirm diagnosis of a symptomatic individual. Such disorders as cancer and heart disease may have genetic as well as environmental causes, and genetic testing may indicate a predisposition for these diseases.

Carrier: Identifies people who carry one copy of a gene mutation that may cause a genetic disorder if coupled with another copy. Three common tests for carrier genes include those for cystic fibrosis, Tay-Sachs disease, and sickle-cell trait. Couples with a history of recessive genetic disorders who are considering having children are commonly tested for carrier genes.

Prenatal: Detects changes in a fetus's genes or chromosomes before birth. Down syndrome is a common genetic disease screened by this method.

Predictive or Presymptomatic: Detects gene mutations that increase a person's risk of developing disorders with a genetic basis or determines if a person will develop a genetic disorder before any symptoms appear. Diseases that may have a genetic and environmental cause may be detected with this test, including such conditions as heart disease, Alzheimer's disease, and adult-onset cancers.

These tests can help you make important decisions about lifestyle and health care. A positive test can mean several things: the laboratory found a certain change in a particular gene, chromosome, or protein, which may indicate that you are the carrier of a certain genetic mutation; the test identified that you are at increased risk of developing a certain disease; or a positive result might simply suggest the need for further testing. A negative test means that the laboratory did not find any changes in the gene, chromosome, or protein under consideration. Because everyone has common variations in their DNA, a negative test may not be considered useful unless it is associated with findings of similar mutations in other individuals; it may be necessary to test other family members for similar mutations to more accurately determine the occurrence of a genetic risk factor.

Treating Disease with Genetic Testing

Cancer is a complex disease that comes in many forms. According to experts at the City of Hope (a designated Comprehensive Cancer Center), cancer is not one disease, but rather hundreds of them. In some forms of cancer, examination of tissues for specific genes and molecular processes can suggest the causes of the cancer, its potential growth, and ways of treating it. Lung cancer, colon cancer, breast cancer—these are all diseases that no longer have to be treated in the same way in every patient because of the new personalized medicine offered by genetic and molecular testing. Within each type of cancer there may be seven or eight different subgroups, each with a different method of treatment. With the advent of personalized medicine, for example, one type of breast cancer may be treated entirely differently from another type of breast cancer.

Lung cancer, which claims one hundred and sixty two thousand lives a year, is one area in which rapid advances are being made. At the M. D. Anderson Cancer Center in Houston, lung cancer patients are being specifically and individually matched to the most suitable treatment for them. Breast cancer will strike one out of every eight women during their lifetimes. Although environmental factors have been determined to increase a woman's risk over genetic ones, several known genetic mutations are linked to the occurrence in families with a history of breast cancer—these genetic factors account for 40 to 51 percent of the risk for breast cancer. About seven hundred and fifty thousand women in the U.S.—about one-half of 1 percent—carry the known gene for breast cancer risk, which has also been linked to ovarian cancer. If your family has a history of breast cancer, you should consider being tested for this gene. A gene linked to melanoma, one of the most aggressive and life-threatening forms of skin cancer, is currently being studied by genetic scientists: researchers at the University of Colorado and Source MDx are now developing blood biomarkers in order to diagnose and screen patients for malignant melanoma. Early detection of melanoma is crucial, so the use of these biomarkers to screen for this disease will have a huge impact on its diagnosis and treatment.

We all know someone who can eat a tremendous amount of food and not gain weight—and the explanation may be in their genes: genetic factors contribute 64 to 84 percent to differences in BMI, or obesity. Genetic testing could help you determine whether you have a marker for obesity, and this information could not only help you to understand your problem, but also aid in choosing the best treatment option as well.

There are those who do not want to know if they are at risk for certain health problems. For these people, not knowing may be a choice that will allow a very preventable or treatable disease to progress beyond treatment. I appreciate that knowing you are at risk for heart disease may be scary, but if you are given this knowledge soon enough, simple lifestyle changes may save your life.

There are large medical organizations and some states that do not want you to have the right to know your own health risks. Why? Are they afraid that you will take charge of your own life and do what is right for you? You deserve to know if you want to. Think about scientific advances as opportunities to become involved with the future of medicine. Within less than a decade, genetic testing will be routine and most likely required. Why should we pay to treat diseases when simple testing will allow for their prevention?

We are in the very early stages of genetic testing, and the sophistication will only increase in the next few years. I chose a company called 23andMe® to perform my genetic test—for less than $400 I now have a very good idea about how to manage my personal health risks. Following are lists of tests taken from the 23andMe Web site. One of the lists shows tests in which this particular company has a high level of confidence in the results; also included are those about which we have a good understanding but for which more research needs to be done.

Genetic Testing Results Widely Regarded as Reliable Based Upon Clinical Evidence

Age-related Macular Degeneration

Alcohol Flush Reaction

Bitter Taste Perception

Celiac Disease

Crohn's Disease

Cystic Fibrosis

Earwax Type

Eye Color

G6PD Deficiency

Lactose Intolerance

Malaria Resistance
(Duffy Antigen)

Muscle Performance

Non-ABO Blood Groups

Norovirus Resistance

Parkinson's Disease

Prostate Cancer

Psoriasis

Resistance to HIV/AIDS

Rheumatoid Arthritis

Sickle Cell Anemia and Malaria Resistance

Type 1 Diabetes

Type 2 Diabetes

Venous Thromboembolism

Genetic Testing Results That Require Additional Clinical Evidence

Alcohol Dependence

Ankylosing Spondylitis

Antidepressant Response

Asthma

Atrial Fibrillation

Attention-Deficit Hyperactivity Disorder

Avoidance of Errors

Back Pain

Baldness

Beta-Blocker Response

Bipolar Disorder

Birth Weight

Blood Glucose

Breast Cancer

C-reactive Protein Level

Caffeine Metabolism

Cluster Headaches

Colorectal Cancer

Creutzfeldt-Jakob Disease

Developmental Dyslexia

Endometriosis

Esophageal Cancer

Food Preference

Freckling

Gallstones

Glaucoma

Gout

HDL Cholesterol Level

HIV Progression

Hair Color

Heart Attack

Height

Heroin Addiction

High Blood Pressure (Hypertension)

Kidney Disease

Larynx Cancer

continued

Longevity

Lou Gehrig's Disease (ALS)

Lung Cancer

Lupus (Systemic Lupus Erythematosus)

Male Infertility

Measures of Intelligence

Memory

Multiple Sclerosis

Neuroblastoma

Nicotine Dependence

Obesity

Obsessive-Compulsive Disorder

Odor Detection

Oral and Throat Cancer

Osteoarthritis

Pain Sensitivity

Peripheral Arterial Disease

Persistent Fetal Hemoglobin

Placental Abruption

Preeclampsia

Progressive Supranuclear Palsy

Restless Legs Syndrome

Schizophrenia

Sjögren's Syndrome

Skin Cancer

Stomach Cancer

Tardive Dyskinesia

Uterine Fibroids

19q13.1   carcinoembryonic antig

19q13.1   B-cell lymphoma

19q13.2   Ectopic CAS

19q13.2   Lutheran blood groop

19q13.2   poliovirus receptor

19q13.2   translocase

19q13.2 ■ apolipoprotein E

19q13.2   apo

19q13.2   apolip

19q13.2   apoli

19q13.2   apolip

19q13.3

Alzheime

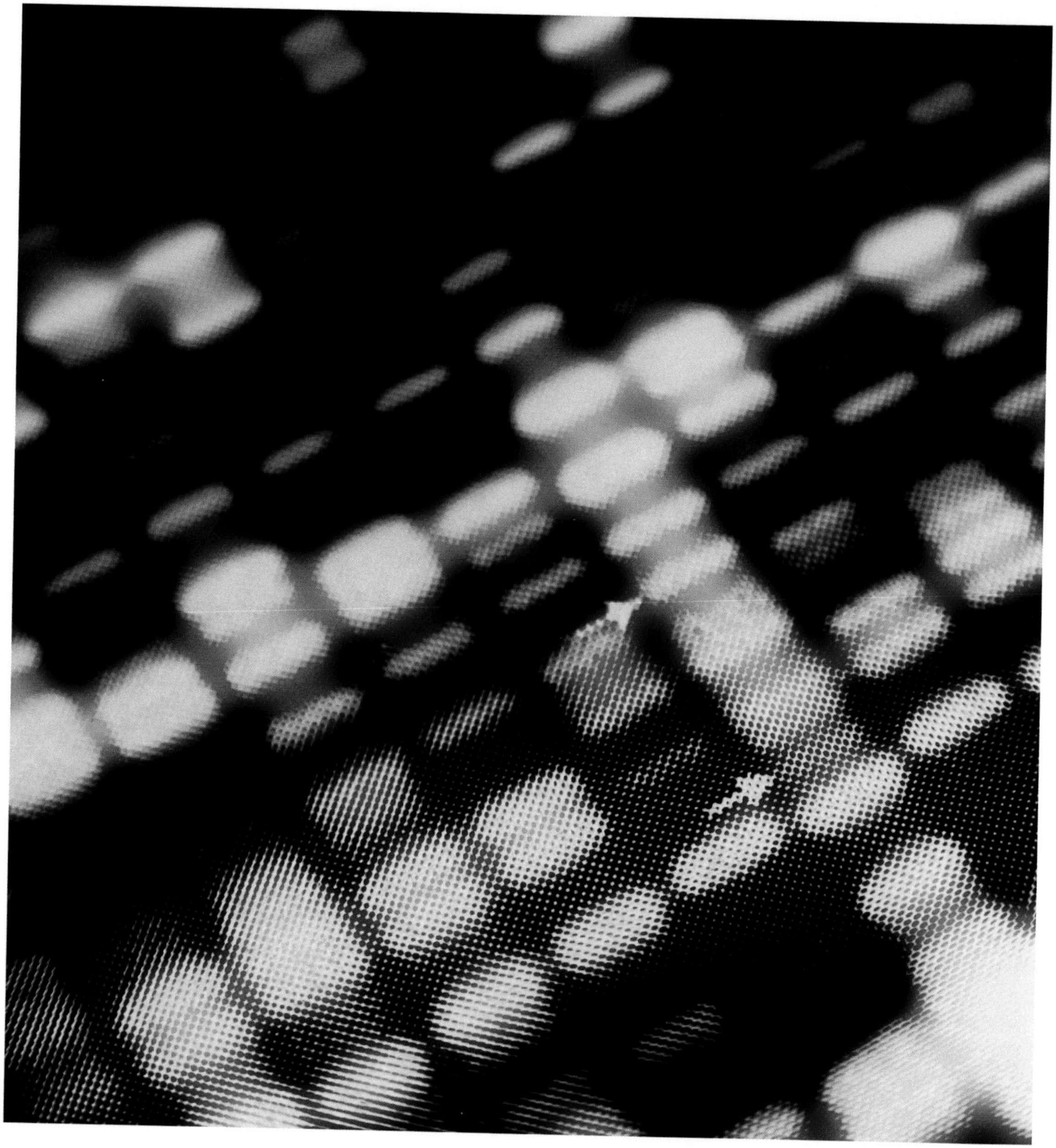

I found 23andMe to be a very good company to work with. The results I got from them provided a lot of detail, and from that information I was able to put together my own health plan. Perhaps because I am a scientist, I want to know for myself. I am personally very glad that I made the choice to have a genetic test. But it is up to you—genetic testing is just one more way to take control of your health. You can weigh the option of performing certain tests based on your own specific genetic risk factors. The cost of genetic testing can range from under $200 to more than $3,000. The tests can be performed on tissues such as those found in saliva, blood, hair, or skin. You may need to consult your insurance company before getting a risk analysis to find out if it's covered by your policy.

Even though genetic testing can provide important information about your health, there has been a reluctance on the part of some to undergo DNA testing because the information gleaned from such tests may be used by insurance companies and employers to screen for people at high risk for certain diseases. In 2008 the Genetic Information Nondiscrimination Act (GINA) was signed; this federal legislation bans insurance companies and employers from discriminating against individuals based on differences in DNA that may affect health. The law does not cover issues such as life insurance, disability insurance, or long-term care insurance. It also does not affect any state legislation—which may vary from state to state—on genetic discrimination that may already be in place. For more information about privacy issues, visit the Web site of the National Human Genome Research Institute (www.genome.gov), which provides detailed information about current legislation.

There are important differences between research testing and clinical genetic testing. Research testing is done to discover previously unknown genes and how they work; the results are usually not available to patients. Clinical testing is done specifically for an individual or family to determine the likelihood of an inherited disorder. While clinical genetic testing is particularly important for those of you who know you are at high risk for inherited diseases, it is not just recommended for high-risk individuals—everyone can benefit from knowing the results of a gene test. A positive test can help you make choices about your future: for example, if you test positive for being at high risk to develop colon cancer, you now have a choice about what to do about it. The chances of surviving this disease are greatest if it is caught early, so you now know that you should have regular colonoscopies to check for the earliest signs of cancer; you may even want to consider colon surgery.

At the very least, these tests give you more information so that you can opt to make simple changes in your lifestyle which will allow you to live a healthy and disease-free life, whether this means choosing high-fiber or low-fat foods or simply adding more activity to your daily routine. Knowledge is power: Knowing your genetic profile may save your life. Armed with this information, you can take that trip to the Fountain of Youth faster than you ever imagined.

TEN STEPS I AM TAKING ON MY JOURNEY TO GOOD HEALTH

Made a decision to focus on health care rather than disease care

Decided to focus on the good news in medicine

Went to the library and checked out a book on the future of health care

Looked into possible alternatives to drug treatment for cardiovascular disease

Went online at 23andme.com and read about genetic testing

Made a chart of my family's medical history and determined
my predisposition to certain diseases

Inquired about pre-symptomatic genetic testing

Checked into my insurance plan's coverage of genetic testing

Called my local state representative to inquire about current
legislation on genetic testing privacy laws

Chose to take control of my medical destiny